EVERYDAY GUIDES
MADE EASY

CODING
HTML & CSS
BASICS

This is a **FLAME TREE** book

First published 2015

Publisher and Creative Director: Nick Wells
Project Editor: Polly Prior
Art Director and Layout Design: Mike Spender
Digital Design and Production: Chris Herbert
Copy Editor: Anna Groves
Technical Editor: Adam Crute
Screenshots: Frederic Johnson and Adam Crute

Special thanks to: Laura Bulbeck, Adam Crute, Josie Mitchell

This edition first published 2015 by
FLAME TREE PUBLISHING
Crabtree Hall, Crabtree Lane
Fulham, London SW6 6TY
United Kingdom

www.flametreepublishing.com

15 17 19 18 16
1 3 5 7 9 10 8 6 4 2

© 2015 Flame Tree Publishing

ISBN 978-1-78361-392-2

Printed in China

All non-screenshot pictures are courtesy of Shutterstock and © the following
photographers: iinspiration 1; baitong333 3; ra2studio 5; scyther5 16;
marekuliasz 8, 40; Ai825 10; gdainti 13 & 15, 52; Syda Productions 19;
patpitchaya 20, 111; MoneyRender 23; Monkey Business Images 24;
GlebStock 26; fotogestoeber 29; ronstik 34; Raywoo 38; Miha Perosa 41;
billdayone 43; Sergey Nivens 48, 110; wavebreakmedia 55, 84, 120; Hamara 58;
Andrey_Popov 60; Ai825 63; Rawpixel 64; winui 67; everything possible 70;
Chukcha 72; baranq 75; Ingvar Bjork 83; Antonio Gravante 86; lassedesignen 94;
3d brained 99; alphaspirit 105; agsandrew 106; MPFphotography 119.

EVERYDAY GUIDES
MADE EASY

CODING
HTML & CSS
BASICS

FREDERIC JOHNSON
& ADAM CRUTE

FLAME TREE
PUBLISHING

CONTENTS

SERIES FOREWORD 5

INTRODUCTION 6

ALL ABOUT HTML AND CSS. 8

New to coding? Then this introduction to HTML and CSS is a must-read.

GETTING STARTED 34

Get to grips with HTML tags, the essential backbone of any website,
and also with CSS, which creates the look of the website.

CREATING WEBSITES 64

Learn how to plan, build and style a website, get it online and also how
to make use of WordPress.

IMAGES, VIDEO AND OTHER ENHANCEMENTS . . . 86

By adding images, audio and video to your site, you will take it to another level.
Learn how to do that here.

ADVANCED CODING 106

Go beyond the basics with HTML5, create animation with CSS keyframes,
get the lowdown on JavaScript and learn what to do if things go wrong.

USEFUL WEBSITES AND FURTHER READING 126

INDEX 127

SERIES FOREWORD

We live in a connected world. We share news, stories and images; our noblest aspirations and darkest nightmares (not to mention rather a lot of cat pictures) criss-cross the globe at an ever-increasing rate, whilst our appetite to consume this infinite variation of human thought (and cute cat pictures) seems boundless.

The conduit for all of this information, the pipes through which the data flows – the enchanted loom through which global culture intertwines and advances – is the internet. Learning to speak the language of the internet, then, is both empowering and rewarding.

Many people believe that programming is hard to learn; nothing could be further from the truth. If you know that 1 + 2 = 3, and that you have to open the fridge door **before** you take out the milk, then you can program!

Of course, mastering any language – human or computer – requires dedicated study over an extended period of time. But just as it's simple to learn enough French to communicate with the locals on a holiday to Paris, so it is easy to get to grips with the basics of most computer languages.

The language of the internet – HTML, CSS and JavaScript – is amongst the simplest languages one can learn, as well as being the most useful and ubiquitous. This book is only an introduction to this language, yet will empower you with the ability to create your own vibrant and exciting websites from scratch.

Don't be scared, it's easy. Turn the page and see for yourself...

Adam Crute

INTRODUCTION

Nowadays, everyone uses the internet, from hobbyists to big business. If you want to promote yourself, a product or simply let people know about your passion, a website gives you a window on the world. It is the go-to destination to find out more information about absolutely anything.

NEED TO KNOW

Now you know why you need a website, how do you go about building one? The core technologies behind every site on the web are HTML (HyperText Markup Language) and

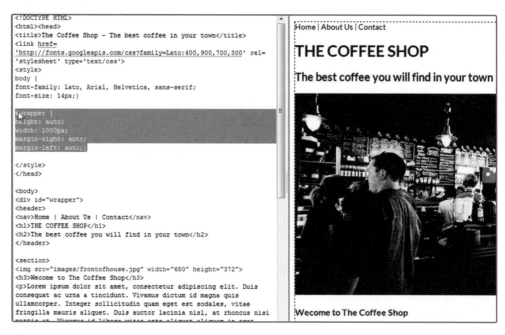

Above: Learn how to turn code into internet gold; creating your own website might not be as hard as you first imagined.

CSS (Cascading Style Sheets). This book reveals exactly how they work, what they can do and, more importantly, shows you how to create your very own website.

GO FURTHER

The advice doesn't stop at simply creating your website: learn how to get your website onto the internet, find out how you can buy your very own .com name, create a blog with WordPress and discover some advanced CSS techniques.

STEP-BY-STEP

The process of a building a website can seem like a daunting task. But this book rises to the challenge and demonstrates the process through a selection of step-by-step guides. These provide easy-to-follow instructions which will guide you through some of the most important building blocks of a website.

EXPERT GUIDANCE

Should all not go according to plan, our helpful troubleshooting guide will help get you back on track, and our Further Reading guide will point you in the direction of where to go next.

CODE EXAMPLES

When showing examples of HTML and CSS code we will use text that looks `like this`. When we want to indicate that something would be written in a code block but that we haven't shown it in the example, we would bold the text as well, like this: `header` **`{style rule}`**. You wouldn't type 'style rule' into the code – rather, we're showing you where the style rule would go.

> ## Hot Tip
>
> **In addition to the more substantial step-by-steps, there is a collection of Hot Tip guides. These offer quick, handy hints and advice to add flourishes to the final website.**

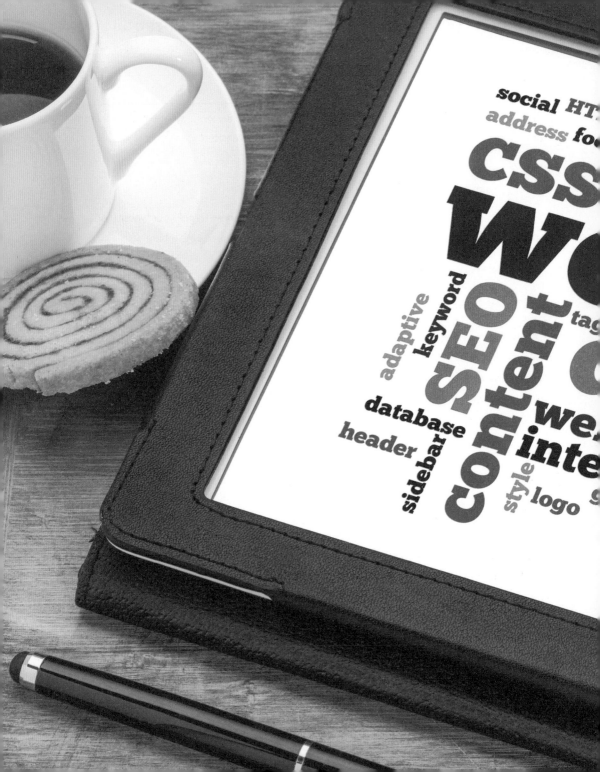

AN INTRODUCTION TO HTML

HTML is the most important component for building websites, web apps and anything else that's delivered via the web. But what is it and what does it do?

WHAT IS HTML?

HTML, or HyperText Markup Language to give it its official title, is the framework upon which all websites are built. If a website were a house, HTML would be the bricks and mortar.

HTML consists of **elements**, the bricks in our hypothetical house. An element starts and ends with something called a **tag** – the mortar, if you will. There are many different elements, each of which has a specific intended use. For example, the video element is used to – can you guess? – yes, place a video on a web page. When your choices of elements are put together in a suitable order you have a web page!

```
1   <h1>HTML is a collection of elements</h1>
2   <h2>These elements are demarked by tags</h2>
3   <p>Each element has a name - it is included in the tag</p>
4   <p>Whatever appears between the opening and closing tags is the content of the element</p>
5
```

Above: HTML is made up of elements, demarked by tags.

WHAT DOES HTML LOOK LIKE?

HTML is nothing more than plain text. If we were creating the aforementioned video element we would write an **opening tag**, `<video>`, and a matching **closing tag**, `</video>`. As you can see, the opening tag starts with '<', states the element name, and then finishes with '>'. The closing tag follows the same pattern, but we insert a '/' before the element name. When a web browser encounters this element it creates a video player on the page. Simple, huh?

What's Inside An Element

So, what goes between those tags? In most circumstances the answer is text and/or other elements. This means that HTML has a nested structure of elements within elements. Incidentally, many developers indent lines of code to reflect this nesting.

```
1    <!DOCTYPE HTML>
2
3    <html>
4
5        <head>
6            <title>My Page</title>
7        </head>
8
9        <body>
10           <header>
11               <h1>A Page All About Me</h1>
12           </header>
13
14           <section>
15               <h2>What I'm thinking now</h2>
16                   <p>Lorem ipsum dolor sit amet, consectetuer adipiscing elit. Sed sagittis ante malesuada velit.
     Curabitur suscipit. Suspendisse quis nibh aliquam sem pulvinar sollicitudin. Etiam venenatis. Curabitur
     luctus.</p>
17                   <p>Nunc venenatis lacus molestie sapien. Maecenas elementum aliquet velit. Ut eget mauris sed leo
     scelerisque lacinia. Nunc arcu magna, mollis id, ornare ac, pharetra sit amet, purus. Aliquam luctus
     consectetuer dolor.</p>
18           </section>
19
20       </body>
21
22   </html>
23
```

Above: Indenting lines of code highlights the nested structure of your elements.

MODIFYING ELEMENTS

Whilst all HTML elements have an intended use, nearly all can be modified in various ways too. For example, we may want to change the dimensions of a video player or the font size of a heading.

Elements are modified by adjusting the **attributes** of the element, and this is done in the opening tag:

```
<video width="720" height="360">
```

As you can see, an attribute name is declared within the opening tag, is followed by '='
and then a **value** wrapped inside quote marks.

Components of HTML

- **Element**: The basic building block of HTML.

- **Tag**: Defines the start and end of an element.

- **Attribute**: Modifies the behaviour and appearance of an element.

Hot Tip

When using quote marks in HTML you can use single ' or double ",
but it is vital to be consistent in which you use.

```
15
16      <video width="640" width="360" src="vids/introvid.mp4"> </video>
17
18      <section lang="en">
19          <article id="article_01">
20              <h2 class="underlinedText">Lorem ipsum dolor sit amet</h2>
21              <p class="redText">Sed sagittis ante malesuada velit. Curabitur suscipit.</p>
22          </article>
23      </section>
24
25
```

Above: Attributes allow you to modify an element.

DOING THINGS WITH STYLE

In old versions of HTML a plethora of different attributes existed for controlling the visual appearance of elements. What's more, different elements had wildly varying sets of attributes that they recognized. Remembering all of the connotations and variations was a nightmare, and so the style attribute was developed.

Obey The Rules

The value assigned to a style attribute is called a **style rule** and this consists of one or more **style commands**. A style command is a pairing of a **style property** and a value to be applied to that property, for example:

```
<body style="color:green; font-weight:bold;">.
```

Each style property name (color and font-weight in this example) is followed by a colon ':', then the value to be assigned to that property, and finally a semicolon ';'.

```
8
9     <body>
10
11        <header style="font-size:18px; color:blue;">
12            <h1 style="font-weight:bold;">HTML and CSS Basics</h1>
13            <h2 style="font-size:14px;">Learn the language of the Internet</h2>
14        </header>
15
16        |
17        <video width="640" width="360" src="vids/introvid.mp4"></video>
18
```

Above: The style attribute allows you to add inline styling to an element.

AN INTRODUCTION TO CSS

If HTML is the bricks and mortar of a house, then CSS provides the decoration. The language is simple but packs a big punch, and without it your web pages would look awful.

WHAT IS CSS?

We've already looked at adding a style rule to an element's `style` attribute. This is called **Inline** styling – it works, but has an inherent problem: if you want to change, say, the font of all of your text headings then you have to edit the `font-family` style property in *every* occurrence of a heading element. This is where **CSS** comes into the picture.

```
 2
 3   <html>
 4
 5     <head>
 6        <title>All About HTML</title>
 7     </head>
 8
 9     <body>
10
11        <header style="font-size:18px; color:blue;">
12           <h1 style="font-weight:bold;">HTML and CSS Basics</h1>
13           <h2 style="font-size:14px;">Learn the language of the
Internet</h2>
14        </header>
15
16
```

HTML and CSS Basics

Learn the language of the Internet

Lorem ipsum dolor sit amet

Sed sagittis ante malesuada velit. Curabitur suscipit. Suspendisse quis nibh aliquam sem pulvinar sollicitudin. Etiam venenatis! Curabitur luctus. Nunc venenatis lacus molestie sapien. Maecenas elementum aliquet velit. Ut eget mauris sed leo scelerisque lacinia. Nunc arcu magna, mollis id, ornare ac, pharetra sit amet, purus. Aliquam luctus consectetuer dolor. In placerat, diam et suscipit posuere, lacus orci vestibulum libero, vulputate faucibus felis leo sit amet elit. Sed hendrerit felis non urna. Donec interdum dui at est. Pellentesque sit amet urna et nunc lobortis egestas. Vestibulum et orci.

```
 3   <html>
 4
 5     <head>
 6        <title>All About HTML</title>
 7     </head>
 8
 9     <body>
10
11        <header style="font-size:24px; color:red;">
12           <h1 style="font-weight:bold;">HTML and CSS Basics</h1>
13           <h2 style="font-size:14px; background-color:black;">
Learn the language of the Internet</h2>
14        </header>
15
16
17
18        <section id="sect1">
19           <article id="article_01" lang="en">
20              <h2 class="italicText">Lorem ipsum dolor sit amet</
```

HTML and CSS Basics

Learn the language of the Internet

Lorem ipsum dolor sit amet

Sed sagittis ante malesuada velit. Curabitur suscipit. Suspendisse quis nibh aliquam sem pulvinar sollicitudin. Etiam venenatis! Curabitur luctus. Nunc venenatis lacus molestie sapien. Maecenas elementum aliquet velit. Ut eget mauris sed leo scelerisque lacinia. Nunc arcu magna, mollis id, ornare ac, pharetra sit amet, purus. Aliquam luctus consectetuer dolor. In placerat, diam et suscipit posuere, lacus orci vestibulum libero, vulputate faucibus felis leo sit amet elit. Sed hendrerit felis non urna. Donec interdum dui at est. Pellentesque sit amet urna et nunc lobortis egestas. Vestibulum et orci.

Above: Making a change to inline style rules can be a fiddly process.

CSS stands for Cascading Style Sheets. It provides the means of separating page content from page appearance, and of applying a style rule to more than one element at a time. A key benefit of this is that any changes made to a CSS style rule will affect all elements that are associated with that rule.

```
25
26    header {
27        position:relative;
28        width:1024px;
29        height:130px;
30        margin:0px auto 0px auto;
31        padding:0px;
32        background-color:#778081;
33        border:none;
34        border-bottom:2px solid #FD5F12;
35    }
36
37    nav {
38        position:relative;
39        width:788px;
40        height:30px;
41        margin:0px auto 0px auto;
42        padding:0px 118px 0px 118px;
43        background-color:#D9D9D9;
44        border:none;
45        border-bottom:1px solid #FD5F12;
46    }
47
```

Above: CSS code comprises selectors and style rules. Notice how indenting the code assists with legibility.

WHAT DOES CSS LOOK LIKE?

Like HTML, CSS is plain text written with a specific structure. CSS code is comprised of **selectors** that identify the HTML element(s) that the subsequent style rule will be applied to. The style rule itself is wrapped in curly brackets, '{' and '}'.

Selection of Selectors

Selectors can take a number of different forms, but in this book we will only focus on three of them: **Type**, **ID** and **Class** selectors. The simplest of these is the Type selector (we'll return to the others later). It consists of nothing more than the name of the HTML element that will receive the selector's style rule. For example, a p selector will target all instances of <p> elements.

WHY CASCADING?

When writing HTML we create a nested structure in which every element is nested within another element. This means that every element has a **parent** element – the element in which a given element is nested – and most elements have **child** element(s), i.e., the element(s) nested within a given element.

```
12
13
14      <section>
15          <h3>Lorem Ipsum</h3>
16      </section>
17
18
```

Above: HTML's nested structure is expressed in terms of ancestry. Here `<h3>` is the child of `<section>`, and `<section>` is the parent of `<h3>`.

When a web browser **renders** (draws) an element in a web page, it has to assess which style rule to apply to that element. But what if it were rendering an element that displays text, such as `<h3>`, but no `font-family` property had been defined in the style rule applied to that element – how does the browser determine which font to use? The answer is that it looks to the parent element and copies the `font-family` property from there.

If a parent element also lacks a specific style property then that property would be inherited from the parent's parent, and so on. Ultimately we have a 'cascade' of style properties in which a property applied to one element will be inherited by the children of that element, unless a child specifically overrides it with a new rule of its own. When this happens the properties of the new rule are passed into the inheritance chain.

Hot Tip

The structure of CSS is simple, but beware: CSS is unforgiving of mistakes.

Components of CSS

○ **Selector**: Targets the HTML element(s) that style rules will be applied to.

○ **Style command**: Specifies a style property and assigns a value to it (aka a 'property-value pair').

○ **Style rule**: A collection of style properties and their associated values.

Right: A complete CSS style sheet containing multiple selectors and style rules.

```
1
2   body {
3       position:relative;
4       background-color:#FD5F12;
5       margin:0px;
6       padding:0px;
7       width:100%;
8       height:100%;
9   }
10
11  #pageBgFill {
12      position:fixed;
13      width:1024px;
14      left:0px;
15      right:0px;
16      top:0px;
17      bottom:0px;
18      margin:0px auto 0px auto;
19      background-color:#D9D9D9;
20  }
21
22  header {
23      position:relative;
24      width:1024px;
25      height:130px;
26      margin:0px auto 0px auto;
27      padding:0px;
28      background-color:#778081;
29      border:none;
30      border-bottom:2px solid #FD5F12;
31  }
32
33  nav {
34      position:relative;
35      width:788px;
36      height:30px;
37      margin:0px auto 0px auto;
38      padding:0px 118px 0px 118px;
39      background-color:#D9D9D9;
40      border:none;
41      border-bottom:1px solid #FD5F12;
```

ESSENTIAL ELEMENTS

As we have learned, an HTML document is made up of a structure of elements, each of which performs a certain role. This document acts like a set of instructions for a web browser, telling it what to draw where. Let's look at the essential elements required by all documents.

THE DOCTYPE DECLARATION

There are a couple of different dialects of HTML that are currently in use – HTML5, the most up-to-date, and XHTML. This book is concerned only with the former, so suffice to say that

```
1   <!DOCTYPE HTML>
2
3
4
5
```

Above: All HTML documents start with a DOCTYPE declaration; this is the declaration for HTML5.

XHTML exists and isn't drastically different from HTML5 – in fact you'd struggle to notice the difference if you didn't know what to look for!

A web browser, however, *has* to be able to tell the difference so that it knows how to render the page. To this end *all* HTML documents start with a **DOCTYPE** declaration. HTML5's declaration is `<!DOCTYPE HTML>`. This easy-to-remember declaration must appear at the top of every HTML5 web page that you create.

THE HTML ELEMENT

If all elements have a parent element then somewhere down the chain there must be a progenitor or starting point; this is the special `<html>` element. All HTML documents include one – and only one – such element. All of the other elements that comprise the web page are nested within this `<html>` element.

```
1  <!DOCTYPE HTML>
2
3  <html>
4
5  </html>
6
7
8  |
```

Above: All HTML documents contain one `<html>` element: no more, no less.

```
1   <!DOCTYPE HTML>
2
3   <html>
4
5       <head>
6
7       </head>
8
9       <body>
10
11      </body>
12
13  </html>
14
```

Above: The <html> element always contains a <head> and a <body> element.

HEAD AND BODY ELEMENTS

The special <html> element always has two child elements, no more, no less: <head> and <body>, in that order. Without these two elements a web page will not work properly (if at all).

The <head> element contains information about the web page, such as its title (shown at the top of the browser window), the text that will appear in search listings, links to other resources, and so on. Nothing within the <head> is rendered into the visible part of the web page.

The <body> element takes care of the actual visible content of your page, i.e. the elements that produce visual output on the rendered web page. Typically you add elements to the <body> in the layout order they will appear on-screen.

CODE COMMENTS

Practically all programming languages provide a facility for adding **comments** to your code, and HTML is no different. Their main use is to add notes, explanations and reminders inside a document, all of which will be ignored by the browser. They can be especially important if you are working on a large website and/or are collaborating with other developers. Best practice, then, is to use comments liberally and freely – you'll be glad you did if you ever have to revisit a page you wrote months previously. An HTML comment looks like this:

```
<!-- This is an HTML comment -->.
```

Hot Tip

Use comments to disable a line or section of code without having to delete it altogether. This really helps when experimenting with ideas or bug hunting.

```
5     <head>
6
7         <!--TO DO: Come up with a better title for the page -->
8         <title>My Page</title>
9     </head>
10
11    <body>
12        <header>
13            <h1>A Page All About Me</h1>
14        </header>
15
16        <section>
17            <h2>What I'm thinking now</h2>
18
19            <!-- Placeholder text...-->
20            <p>Lorem ipsum dolor sit amet, consectetuer adipiscing elit. Sed sagittis ante malesuada velit.
   Curabitur suscipit. Suspendisse quis nibh aliquam sem pulvinar sollicitudin. Etiam venenatis. Curabitur
   luctus.</p>
21
22            <!--This next element is 'commented-out' -->
23
24            <!--<p>Nunc venenatis lacus molestie sapien. Maecenas elementum aliquet velit. Ut eget mauris sed
   leo scelerisque lacinia. Nunc arcu magna, mollis id, ornare ac, pharetra sit amet, purus. Aliquam luctus
   consectetuer dolor.</p>-->
25
26        </section>
27
28    </body>
29
```

Above: Comments are invaluable: the more the merrier!

HOW TO USE CSS

Before delving any deeper into CSS we need to establish how to include it in an HTML document. There are two ways to do this.

EMBEDDED STYLE SHEETS

An **embedded** style sheet is one where all of the selectors and style rules appear in the <head> element of the HTML document they apply to. This is done by creating a <style> element (or elements, under some circumstances) within the page's <head> element.

You then type the desired selectors and style rules inside this <style> element. This approach has the advantage of keeping all of the code for a page – HTML and CSS – within a single file, but can become difficult to manage for larger sites comprising many pages.

```
5    <head>
6        <title>My Page</title>
7
8        <style>
9            body {
10               font-family:Arial, Helvetica, sans-serif;
11               font-size:14px;
12               color:black;
13           }
14           h1 {
15               font-size:24px;
16               font-weight:bold;
17           }
18           h2 {
19               font-size:18px;
20               font-weight:bold;
21               color:gray;
22           }
23           p {
24               margin-top:6px;
25               margin-bottom:6px;
26           }
27       </style>
28
29   </head>
30
```

Above: Embedded style sheets are nested within the <head> of a document.

EXTERNAL STYLE SHEETS

With an **external** style sheet, the CSS code is written in a separate file and then linked to any HTML documents you wish to apply the style sheet to. A CSS document is simply a plain text file, typically saved with a '.css' filename extension.

Linking CSS Documents to HTML Documents

An external style sheet is associated with an HTML page using a `<link>` element placed in the `<head>` of the page:

```
<link type="text/css" rel="stylesheet"
href="myCssDocument.css" /> .
```

Notice that the tag for this element is not paired with a closing tag, but includes a '/' before the final angle-bracket. This is commonly known as a self-closing tag or element; the reason it is self-closing is because no other elements can be nested within it.

```
 4
 5      <head>
 6          <title>My Page</title>
 7
 8          <link rel="stylesheet" type="text/css" href="css/siteStyles.css" />
 9
10      </head>
11
```

Above: External style sheets are associated with a web page via a `<link>` element.

There are a few attributes that need to be set: The `type` and `rel` attributes inform the browser what type of data to expect within the targeted document – always use the settings shown above. The `href` attribute defines the location and name of the CSS document itself. Typically this will be located on the same server as the web page, but often within a subfolder of the **site root**. Incidentally, the site root folder on most servers is called 'wwwroot'.

Hot Tip

A website consists of a hierarchy of files and folders, just like the hard disk in your computer. The top level of this hierarchy is known as the site root.

Below: CSS documents are often stored in a subfolder of the website's root folder.

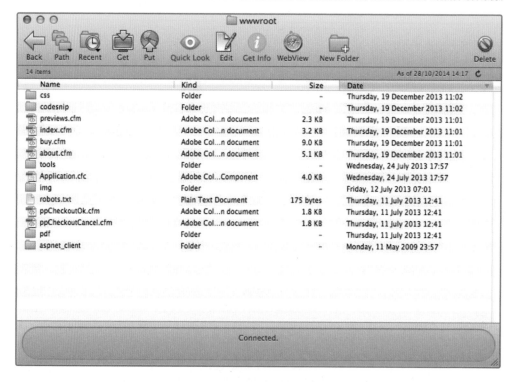

Advantages of External Style Sheets

External style sheets really come into their own when you are building a full website where it is normal for the pages that comprise the site to share a common look and feel. Because external style sheets can be linked to as many HTML pages as you like, they provide a central point from which you can modify and adapt the visual design of your entire site.

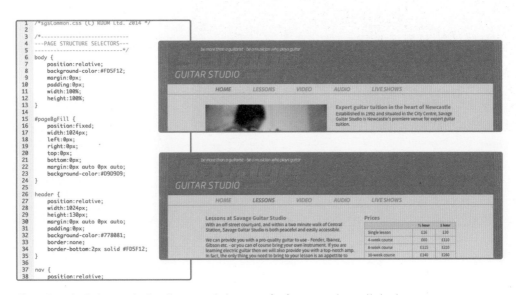

Above: External style sheets can be shared between multiple pages, perfect for common elements like headers.

MULTIPLE STYLE SHEETS

An HTML document can be linked to multiple style sheets. This allows you to arrange your selectors and style rules in logical groupings, with each group saved in a different CSS file. You then only need link a page to the style sheets that it needs.

It's also possible to mix embedded and external style sheets within the same document: style rules relating purely to the document can be embedded, and site-wide style rules can be derived from external style sheets.

Be aware that using multiple sheets increases the risk of applying conflicting values to a style property of an element, so if an element doesn't look as expected then it's worth digging around to check where the problematic style rule(s) is actually coming from.

Methods of Applying Styling

○ **Inline**: A style rule is declared within an element's `style` attribute.

○ **Embedded**: CSS code is written inside a `<style>` element in the `<head>` of an HTML document.

○ **External**: CSS code is written inside a separate text file and associated with an HTML document via a `<link>` element.

```
 5      <head>
 6          <title>My Page</title>
 7
 8          <link rel="stylesheet" type="text/css" href="css/siteStyles.css" />
 9
10          <style>
11              body {
12                  font-family:Arial, Helvetica, sans-serif;
13                  font-size:14px;
14                  color:black;
15              }
16              h1 {
17                  font-size:24px;
18                  font-weight:bold;
19              }
20              h2 {
21                  font-size:18px;
22                  font-weight:bold;
23                  color:gray;
24              }
25              p {
26                  margin-top:6px;
27                  margin-bottom:6px
28              }
29          </style>
30
31      </head>
32
33      <body style="margin-left:20px; margin-right:20px">
34          |
35          <header>
36              <h1>A Page All About Me</h1>
37          </header>
```

Left: The three methods of applying CSS style rules to HTML elements.

NEW FEATURES OF HTML5

HTML5 is still HTML, but it is simply the latest version of the language. It contains many of the elements found in previous versions but also features a number of new elements and rules. In general, when somebody uses the term HTML5, they are referring to these new features.

SEMANTIC ELEMENTS

One of the aims of HTML5 is to introduce clear and consistent semantics into the language, such that the element names convey information about the purpose of an element and where it sits in the logical structure of a document.

Hot Tip

Semantic elements are particularly helpful to the screenreader applications that assist with web browsing for people with visual impairment.

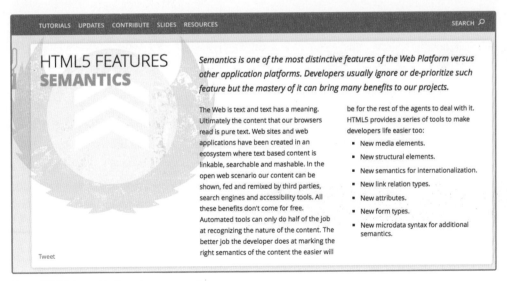

Above: HTML5 places a lot of importance on semantics.

Therefore it includes a new set of elements that satisfies this need for semantic meaning, for example, `<header>`, `<video>`, `<article>` and `<footer>`. The fact that the element names convey exactly what these new elements are for is what makes them semantic.

Above: HTML5 works beautifully on mobile devices.

NEW FUNCTIONALITY

HTML5 introduced a lot of new functionality to web pages that would previously have required third-party plug-ins, such as Adobe Flash Player, to be installed on the end-user's browser. These new features are a breath of fresh air to developers because they make it infinitely simpler to add functionality, such as drag-and-drop, web forms, video, audio, 'live' graphics (including 3D), and much more.

Better for Mobile

Many popular browser plug-ins cannot be installed on mobile operating systems. HTML5 has fixed this by negating the need for many such third-party plug-ins, and so if you expect your web pages to be viewed on mobile devices then HTML5 is the only game in town.

WHAT IS CSS3?

CSS3 is still CSS; it is simply the latest version of the language. This third major version brings with it some important enhancements that make the language much more capable than previously.

VISUAL EFFECTS

One of the main advances in CSS3 is its ability to apply visual effects, such as drop shadow or blur, that would previously need to be produced in an image editor such as Adobe Photoshop. The effects on offer are fairly basic, but they are a godsend to developers who no longer have to jump back and forth between HTML editor and image editor just to put a little shadow on a graphic.

Below: A simple example of a CSS shadow.

Better Backgrounds

Another nifty CSS3 feature is `background-size`. This is a CSS property that allows background images (these being images that sit in the background of an HTML element) to automatically scale as required. By assigning a value to the property, such as `cover`, the image will fill an element's background: simple but effective.

Hot Tip

Just because you can do something doesn't mean you have to: too much eye candy can be as off-putting to visitors as too little.

Animations

The current big thing in CSS is animation. Previously, this was impossible in the browser without the help of third-party plug-ins or extensive scripting (or both), but now designers and developers can create slick and impressive animations with nothing more than CSS code. *See page 100 for more on this.*

Below: Check out this impressive CSS3 animation at http://codepen.io/juliangarnier/pen/idhuG

THE BENEFITS OF UNDERSTANDING HTML AND CSS

HTML and CSS are ubiquitous, and are used widely even outside of web development. As such, possessing an understanding of the languages can give you a considerable professional advantage.

BECOME THE EXPERT

Most companies nowadays have a web presence of some form or another, but many lack the in-house skills to support and maintain their sites properly. Possessing the ability to take on such a role, then, can make you an invaluable employee, especially in smaller businesses.

Below: An in-depth knowledge of CSS means better websites.

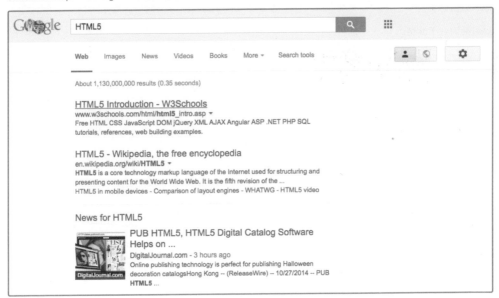

Ch-ch-ch-ch-ch Changes

As well as giving you the ability to problem-solve web pages, having a solid grounding in HTML and CSS provides you with the knowledge to make modifications to a site, confident that you will not break the site in the process.

Keeping up with the Trends

The graphical aspects of web design are heavily influenced by current vogues and trends. Having the ability to keep your site abreast of current fashions, then, ensures it always looks modern and fresh, helping you to build visitor numbers.

Faster Websites

The ability to recognize the right HTML and CSS for the right job can mean the difference between a slick and nimble experience for your visitors, or a slow and frustrating one... guess which they prefer!

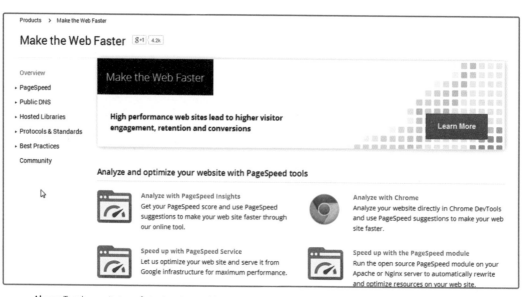

Above: Tweak your site to go faster to get more visitors.

What We've Learned

○ **HTML**: HyperText Markup Language; for constructing web pages.

○ **CSS**: Cascading Style Sheets; for styling web pages.

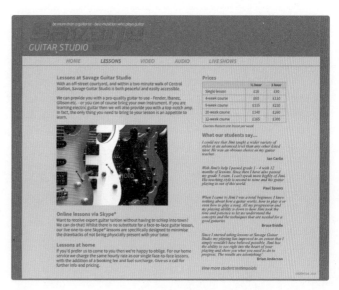

○ **Element**: The building block of HTML.

○ **Tag**: Demarks the start and end of an element.

○ **Attribute**: Provides the means to modify the behaviour and appearance of an element.

○ **Style property**: Assigns a value to a given CSS property.

Above: The various components come together to give a full web page.

○ **Style rule**: A collection of style properties.

○ **Selector**: CSS component that specifies the HTML elements to which a style rule will be applied.

○ **Inline style**: A style rule attached to a single element via the element's `style` attribute.

○ **Embedded style sheet**: A set of style rules grouped by selector; located within a `<style>` element.

○ **External style sheet**: A set of style rules grouped by selector; located within a separate text document.

Homepage</title>

lor=white>

rder="0" cellpadding="10">

g src="images/logo.png">

Hello</h1>

DEMYSTIFYING HTML AND CSS

There is a baffling array of HTML elements and CSS properties that can be brought to bear on a website. Here we will demystify both with a deeper look into some of the essential HTML elements and CSS properties required for building vibrant and attractive websites.

THE BASIC BUILD

If you've been following along and paying attention, you should now know what a web page is, and have a basic understanding of its main building blocks. Now we're going to expand the picture a bit and consider websites. A website is a collection of HTML and CSS documents that are brought together to create a collection of useful content, displayed via an attractive user interface.

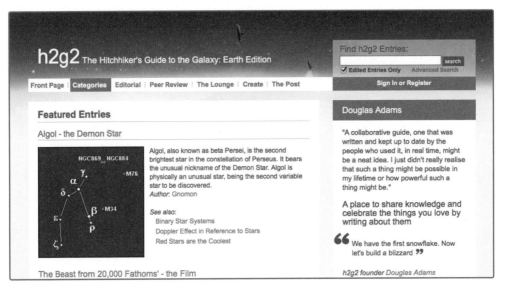

Above: Websites are made up of a number of pages.

Oodles of Elements

We've already discussed what an element is, but what we haven't mentioned is that there are hundreds of them! Don't fear though, you'll find that there is only a handful that you use or need on a regular basis; it is these elements that we'll be discussing over the coming pages.

Above: You can find a full list of elements and descriptions of what they do at http://www.quackit.com/html_5/tags/.

TALKING ABOUT HTML ELEMENTS

We discussed the `<html>`, `<head>` and `<body>` elements in the previous chapter; these are the elements that should form the basic framework of all your web pages. Let's now look at the elements that go within this basic framework.

A FLEXIBLE FRIEND

We're going to start by looking at a slightly unusual element: the `<div>`. What's unusual about it is that it has no specific intended use; it is essentially an empty container that you can use

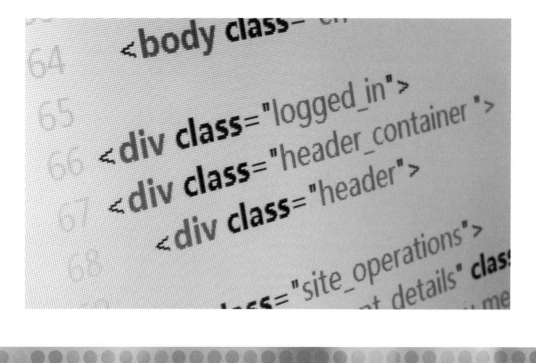

for a variety of purposes. One of the most common uses of a `<div>` is to allow you to group together sets of related elements, such as those that comprise the header of a page.

What's that, you say? You thought there was a `<header>` element in HTML5? Indeed there is, but there is no such thing in XHTML or older versions of HTML. So what did developers do prior to HTML5? To answer that we need to take a small detour...

The ID Attribute

You will recall that elements have attributes that can be assigned a value. One such attribute, available to all visual elements, is `id`. This allows you to provide a unique identifier for a specific element in your page, and is widely used in HTML. To see why, we need to look at what `id` means from the context of CSS.

```
 8
 9     <body>
10
11         <div>
12
13             <header>
14                 <h1>Divs are Containers</h1>
15             </header>
16
17             <div>
18                 <p>Divs can be nested within other divs</p>
19             </div>
20
21         </div>
22
23         <div>
24             <h2>Divs have no semantic meaning</h2>
25         </div>
26
27     </body>
28
```

Above: The `<div>` element is the developer's flexible friend.

Hot Tip

The value assigned to an element's `id` attribute must not be used as the `id` for any other element within the same page.

```
11         <div id="main">
12
13             <header>
14                 <h1>Divs are Containers</h1>
15             </header>
16
17             <div id="contentBlock">
18                 <p>Divs can be nested within other divs</p>
19             </div>
20
21         </div>
22
23         <div id="divComment">
24             <h2>Divs have no semantic meaning</h2>
25         </div>
26
```

Above: The ID attribute gives an element a unique identifier.

```
 6   body {
 7        position:relative;
 8        background-color:#FD5F12;
 9        margin:0px;
10        padding:0px;
11        width:100%;
12        height:100%;
13   }
14
15   #myElement {
16        position:fixed;|
17        width:1024px;
18        left:0px;
19        right:0px;
20        top:0px;
21        bottom:0px;
22        margin:0px auto 0px auto;
23        background-color:#D9D9D9;
24   }
25
```

Above: The ID selector allows a style rule to be targeted at a specific HTML element.

The ID Selector

An ID selector targets the single element whose id attribute value matches the ID selector. An ID selector looks like this:

#myElement {**style rule**}

The '#' (hash) states that this is an ID selector; its style rule will be applied to the HTML element whose id attribute value is "myElement".

What's All Of This Got To Do With <div>?

A <div> element's flexibility is delivered mainly via style properties, for it is these that determine how the <div> will be displayed on screen. So – finally getting back to the earlier question about the pre-HTML5 method of creating a header-like element – the answer is to write the following into the page's HTML:

<div id="header">**content**</div>

And add this to the page's CSS:

#header {**style rule**}

The Semantic Imperative

In HTML5, element names are intended to convey information about the element. For

example, a `<header>` element is intended to display information such as a company name, logo, and a navigation bar, and to be located at the top of the screen; this is self-evident, thanks to the name of the element.

The pre-HTML5 method of creating a page header, discussed above, is *valid* HTML5, but it's not *good* HTML5 because `<div>` conveys no meaning. Yes, an id value of `"header"` conveys meaning, but a developer could just as easily use a value of `"foobar"` – it would make no difference to the ID selector/attribute mechanism, but any semantic meaning would be lost. For this reason, browsers are not allowed to derive semantic meaning from id attributes.

Right: These three elements are valid HTML5 and will deliver identical results, but only one has semantic meaning.

```
8
9        <body>
10
11           <header>
12           </header>
13
14           <div id="header">
15           </div>
16
17           <div id="foobar">
18           </div>
19
20        </body>
21
```

```
8
9       <body>
10          <div id="wrapper">
11
12              <header>
13                  <!--Header content here-->
14              </header>
15
16              <section id="main">
17                  <!--Main page content here-->
18              </section>
19
20              <aside>
21                  <!--Aside content here-->
22              </aside>
23
24              <div id="adPanel">
25                  <!--Advertising content here-->
26              </div>
27
28              <footer>
29                  <div id="copyrightPanel">
30                      <!--Copyright boxout here-->
31                  </div>
32              </footer>
33
34          </div>
35      </body>
36
```

Above: `<div>` elements are unavoidable, but favour HTML5 semantic elements whenever possible.

The `<div>` Imperative

There are those who believe the `<div>` element should be retired because of its lack of a consistent and predictable semantic meaning. In reality the use of `<div>` is unavoidable because HTML5 cannot supply an element for every conceivable structural possibility. Best practice, then, is to only use `<div>` elements where there is no suitable HTML5 alternative. Let's take a look at those alternatives now...

WHAT'S A HEADER?

A `<header>` element is intended to sit at the top of a web page and typically will be the same across all of a site's pages. In general, a page's `<header>` will contain a logo and/or title of the page, and will often include the site navigation menu too.

Hot Tip

`<head>` **and** `<header>` **are separate and unrelated elements.**

WHAT'S A FOOTER?

The <footer> element should be positioned at the bottom of a web page, and is normally the same across all pages on a site. In general it is used for holding copyright information and additional navigation links, but it can contain any elements that you like.

Above: The footer of a website is found at the bottom of the page.

WHAT'S CONTENT?

Content is the main bulk of information and media on your page: it's the stuff that your visitors have come to see! Unlike the `<header>` and `<footer>` elements that tend to be uniform throughout a site, the content area of a page will differ from page to page.

The menu/navigation system on a website is critical to how it works. Take a look at other websites to find one that works well for you and take inspiration from it.

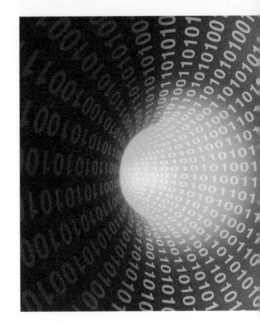

```
1   <!DOCTYPE HTML>
2
3   <html>
4
5       <head>
6           <!--Head used for defining meta data about the page-->
7           <title>All Structural Elements</title>
8       </head>
9
10      <body>
11          <!--Body contains page's visual content-->
12
13          <header>
14              <!--Header content here; One header per page please-->
15              <nav>
16                  <!--Main page navigation control-->
17              </nav>
18          </header>
19
20          <section>
21              <!--A block of page content; Multiple sections allowed-->
22
23              <article>
24                  <!--Article content here; Multiple articles allowed-->
25              </article>
26
27          </section>
28
29          <footer>
30              <!--Footer content here; One footer per page please-->
31              <nav>
32                  <!--Footer navigation menu-->
33              </nav>
34          </footer>
35
36      </body>
37
38  </html>
39
```

Above: Structural elements provide a logical structure into which a page's content is written.

Page Sections

The `<section>` element is meant as a generic container for groups of related content, i.e. for 'sections' of your page. `<section>` elements typically follow the `<header>` element of a page.

OTHER STRUCTURAL ELEMENTS

The `<header>`, `<section>` and `<footer>` elements create both a page structure into which other elements can be placed, and a logical structure for the different types of information within a page. There are four more structural elements in HTML5 that you will use regularly.

Site Navigation

Most websites include a site navigation menu to allow users to move quickly and easily around the site; HTML5 provides the `<nav>` element to contain the elements of such a navigation menu. The `<nav>` element is generally created as a child of `<header>`, but this is not a requirement.

Article Element

The `<article>` element is intended as the final element in a structural chain in that it typically resides within another structural element such as `<section>`. The idea of `<article>` is that its content relates to a single subject, much like an article in a newspaper.

Aside Element

The idea behind an `<aside>` element is for it to display content that's related to content within another structural element, but that s not a direct part of that content. Semantically, any structural element can have a related <aside> element, but the typical usage is as a sidebar for showing things such as adverts, profile information, or links to other areas of the site.

Right: An `<aside>` element is intended for displaying content relating to `<section>` or `<article>` elements.

```
9
10    <body>
11        <!--Body contains page's visual content-->
12
13        <header>
14            <!--Header content here; One header per page please-->
15            <nav>
16                <!--Main page navigation control-->
17            </nav>
18        </header>
19
20        <section>
21            <!--A block of page content; Multiple sections allowed-->
22
23            <article>
24                <!--Article content here; Multiple articles allowed-->
25            </article>
26
27            <aside>
28                <!--Aside content relates to other page content - here
29                it relates to the above article;
30                Multiple asides allowed-->
31            </aside>
32
33        </section>
34
35        <aside>
36            <!--Aside content here-->
37        </aside>
38
39        <footer>
40            <!--Footer content here; One footer per page please-->
41            <nav>
42                <!--Footer navigation menu-->
43            </nav>
44        </footer>
45
46    </body>
47
```

UNDERSTANDING CSS SELECTORS

We've already discussed CSS Type and ID selectors, but there is another important selector you need to know about: the Class selector. It is also possible to combine selectors in various ways; let's take a look.

```
127
128    .italic {
129        font-family:"source_sans_proitalic";
130    }
131
132    .bold {
133        font-family:"source_sans_probold";
134    }
135
136    .footerText {
137        position:absolute;
138        font:10px "source_sans_proregular";
139        color:#787878;
140        right:0px;
141        bottom:6px;
142        width:auto;
143        margin:6px 10px 6px auto;
144        padding:0px;
145    }
146
147    .navbarButton {
148        width:auto;
149        margin-left:4%;
150        margin-right:4%;
151        margin-top:9px;
152        padding:0px;
153        cursor:pointer;
154    }
155
156
157
```

CLASS SELECTORS

Recall that a Type selector targets any HTML elements of matching type, and that an ID selector targets the single HTML element with a matching id attribute value. A Class selector, then, allows you to target a specific *classification* of HTML elements. A Class selector is written like this (notice the '.' which precedes the class name):

.myClassName {**style rule**}

This selector would target any and all HTML elements that had been given the classification of myClassName .

Left: Class selectors target elements via the classification of those elements.

Typed Class Selectors

This can be taken a step further by combining a Class selector with a Type selector, for example, `article.newsStory {`**`style rule`**`}`. This selector would target all `<article>` elements that had been given a classification of `"newsStory"`. But how do we classify an element? Easy...

The Class Attribute

Every visual element has a `class` attribute. Here's how it looks: `<article class="newsStory">`. Once given a classification in this way, the element will receive the style rule associated with the `.newsStory` selector. If the selector had been `p.newsStory` then the above element would not have been selected because it is an `<article>`, not a `<p>`.

Beware: Using Class selectors can increase the risk of conflicting style properties being applied to an element.

```
37
38      <body>
39          <header>
40              <h1>A Page All About Me</h1>
41              <nav class="navbarButton">Home | About Me | Contact</nav>
42          </header>
43
44          <section>
45              <h2 class="bold italic">What I'm thinking now</h2>
46              <p class="italic">Lorem ipsum dolor sit amet, consectetuer adipiscing elit. Sed sagittis ante
        malesuada velit. Curabitur suscipit. Suspendisse quis nibh aliquam sem pulvinar sollicitudin. Etiam venenatis.
        Curabitur luctus.</p>
47                  <p>Nunc venenatis lacus molestie sapien. Maecenas elementum aliquet velit. Ut eget mauris sed leo
        scelerisque lacinia. Nunc arcu magna, mollis id, ornare ac, pharetra sit amet, purus. Aliquam luctus consectetuer
        dolor.</p>
48          </section>
49
50          <footer>
51              <p class="footerText">Cum sociis natoque penatibus et magnis dis parturient montes, nascetur
        ridiculus mus.</p>
52              <p class="footerText">Fusce libero nunc, tempor non, convallis ut, luctus sit amet, lectus.</p>
53          </footer>
54
55      </body>
56
```

Above: Elements can be given classifications via the `class` attribute.

Multiple Classifications

Imagine you have created three different Class selectors in a page's CSS: .boldText, .italicText and .underlinedText, and assigned a suitable style rule to each, such as {font-weight:bold;} etc. This would allow you to classify text-based elements using these class names... but what if you want bold *and* italic text? Simple, just list the class names in the element's class attribute, and separate each class name with a space.

```
2
3
4    <p class="boldText">Lorem ipsum dolor sit amet, consectetuer adipiscing elit.</p>
5    <p class="italicText">Sed sagittis ante malesuada velit.</p>
6    <p class="underlinedText">Curabitur suscipit. Suspendisse quis nibh aliquam sem.</p>
7    <p class="boldText italicText">Pulvinar sollicitudin. Etiam venenatis.</p>
8    <p class="boldText italicText underlinedText">Curabitur luctus.</p>
9
```

Above: An element's class attribute can accept a space-delimited list of class names. All will be applied.

COMPOUND SELECTORS

We've already mentioned one example of a compound selector, often known as a typed class selector, but there are many other ways of combining selectors; let's take a look at a few of them.

Multiple Type Selectors

If you want to create a style rule that will be applied to a number of different elements based on their element type, you can simply list those types in a selector and use a ',' to separate each type name. For example h2, h3, p {**style rule**} will target all <h2>, <h3> and <p> elements.

```
 2
 3
 4   h1, h2, h3 {
 5       font-family:"source_sans_probold";
 6       font-weight:bold;
 7   }
 8
 9   article h2 {
10       color:blue;
11   }
12
13   article p {
14       font-family:"source_sans_regular";
15   }
16
17   nav > p {
18       colour:red;
19       cursor:pointer;
20   }
```

Descendant Selectors

There are times when we want to target an element based upon its position within the nested structure of the HTML. For example, we may want to target all <p> elements that are descended from (i.e. nested within, at any level) an <article> element: article p {**style rule**} (notice the space between the type names in the selector).

Left: CSS has numerous forms of selector.

Child Selectors

A child selector targets elements that are a child of another element (note that a Descendant selector also targets grandchildren, great grandchildren, etc.). So a selector of `article > h3 {style rule}` would target all `<h3>` elements that were direct children of an `<article>` element (notice the '>' between the type names in the selector).

A LOT TO LEARN

CSS is a simple language, but the devil is in the detail – and there's a *lot* of detail, much more than we can cover here. If you want to find out more then check out some of the many great websites and books dedicated to the subject.

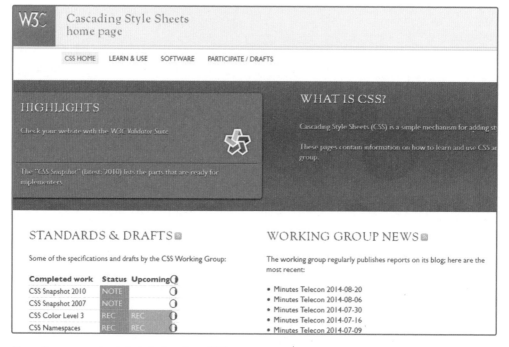

Above: There are many sites dedicated to the subject of CSS.

TEXT-BASED ELEMENTS

Most web pages contain text – often quite a lot of it – and so unsurprisingly there is a collection of elements that are dedicated to displaying text. Text elements tend to be nested within the structural elements that we've discussed previously.

HEADING TEXT

There is a group of HTML elements that is dedicated to displaying headings; their names are very easy to remember. The first is called <h1>, the second <h2> and so on until we reach <h6>.

Hot Tip

<h4> to <h6> are rarely used – just how many levels of heading does one need?!

```
8
9       <body>
10
11          <h1>Heading level 1</h1>
12          <h2>Heading level 2</h2>
13          <h3>Heading level 3</h3>
14          <h4>Heading level 4</h4>
15          <h5>Heading level 5</h5>
16          <h6>Heading level 6</h6>
17
18      </body>
19
```

Above: There are six levels of heading element in HTML.

Heading Levels

The number in the heading element's name represents the 'level' of the heading, in other words how important (and therefore prominent) the heading is. <h1> is the most prominent, and <h6> the least.

Heading Semantics

Prior to HTML5 the different levels of heading represented nothing more than different degrees of visual prominence: <h1> the boldest and largest, <h6> the smallest and lightest. HTML5 goes a step further and imposes semantic meaning on the different heading levels.

Heading level 1

Heading level 2

Heading level 3

Heading level 4

Heading level 5

Heading level 6

Above: <h1> is the most prominent heading, <h6> the least.

The easiest way to explain this is by using the analogy of a book such as the one you are reading now. If a web page were a chapter in a book, then <h1> would be analogous to the chapter title, so <h1> should only appear once in a web page.

<h2> would be analogous to section headings within a chapter, and so can appear more than once after an <h1>. <h3> is analogous to subheadings within a section... and so on. Heading semantics can be tricky, but keep the book analogy in mind – it helps!

Logical Structure of Headings

The semantic nature of HTML5 headings means that they also infer a logical structure. Returning to our book analogy, the parent of a subheading (<h3>) will be a section heading (<h2>), and the parent of a section heading will be a chapter heading (<h1>). But what if you want to create a single heading that has two components: a 'stand-first' and 'tagline', so to speak?

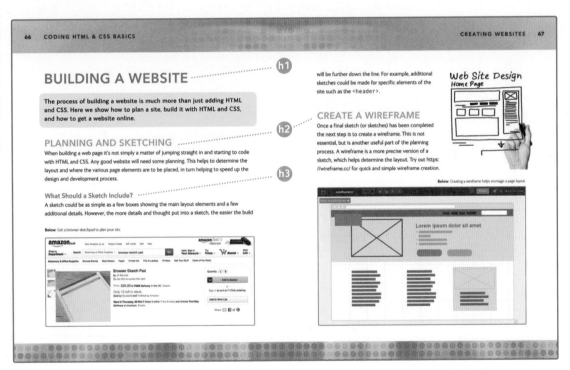

Above: Like the levels of heading in a book, HTML5 headings impart a logical structure on the text, so <h1> can be thought of as a chapter heading, <h2> can be thought of as a section heading and <h3> can be thought of as a sub-section heading.

Heading Groups

We might create a two-part heading like this:

```
<h1>HTML and CSS</h1>
<h2>The Language of the Internet</h2>
```

Unfortunately there's a problem here: the `<h2>` is a subheading of `<h1>`, but as things stand it's denoting a new section in the logical structure of the page. The solution is the `<hgroup>` element; it allows you to group together multiple levels of heading without implying that you are creating new sections in the logical structure – the first heading in the `<hgroup>` is the heading-level that will be inferred. So instead of the above we would write this:

```
<hgroup>
    <h1>HTML and CSS</h1>
    <h2>The Language of the Internet</h2>
</hgroup>
```

Now, the `<h2>` element will be considered part of the `<h1>`, and semantic wellbeing is restored.

```
11
12          <!--Semantically incorrect...:-->
13          <h1>HTML and CSS</h1>
14          <h2>The Language of the Internet</h2>
15
16          <!--Semantically correct...:-->
17          <hgroup>
18              <h1>HTML and CSS</h1>
19              <h2>The Language of the Internet</h2>
20          </hgroup>
21
```

Above: An `<hgroup>` element assists in maintaining semantic accuracy in headings.

PARAGRAPH TEXT

You'll be pleased to know that paragraph text (the main body text of a page) is much simpler than headings. We have just one paragraph element, <p>. Generally a <p> contains only text, but it can also have images and certain other elements embedded within it.

Styling Paragraphs

A common strategy for styling paragraphs is to create a p Type selector in which to define the very basic aspects of your paragraph style, such as the font, and then create a collection of Class selectors that apply specific styling, such as bold text, underlining and italics. You can then assign the desired class name(s) to a given <p> element as required.

```
7
8        <style>
9
10           .boldText {
11               font-weight:bold;
12           }
13
14           .italicText {
15               font-style:italic;
16           }
17
18           .underlinedText {
19               text-decoration:underline;
20           }
21
22        </style>
23
```

```
25
26       <body>
27
28           <p class="boldText">Lorem ipsum dolor sit amet, consectetuer adipiscing elit.</p>
29           <p class="italicText">Sed sagittis ante malesuada velit.</p>
30           <p class="underlinedText">Curabitur suscipit. Suspendisse quis nibh aliquam sem.</p>
31           <p class="boldText italicText">Pulvinar sollicitudin. Etiam venenatis.</p>
32           <p class="boldText italicText underlinedText">Curabitur luctus.</p>
33
34       </body>
35
```

Above: Creating a number of Class selectors containing simple rules makes for easy paragraph styling.

Styling Within a Paragraph

There are many occasions when you will want to change the text format within a paragraph, such as when you wish to emphasize a word or passage with *italic* or **bold** text. There are a few ways to do this: italicizing can be achieved by wrapping a span of text in an <em> (emphasis) element:

```
<p>Mary had a <em>little</em> lamb</p>
```

Or for bold text:

```
<p>It really <b>was</b> a dear</p>
```

A better way, however, is to use the <span> element. It is much more flexible because rather than giving a single style property change, it can apply a whole style rule – or rules – in one go:

> ## Hot Tip
>
> **When adding child elements to a text-based element it is normal to place the new tags within the text without creating new lines or indentation in the code.**

```
<p>But she <span class="redText italic">couldn't tell the difference</span></p>
```

Mary had a *little* lamb

It really **was** a dear

But she *couldn't tell the difference*

Above: Text format changes within a paragraph are easy with the <span> element.

HYPERLINKS

A website would not be a website if it didn't have hyperlinks. They are the mechanism that allow web browsing to happen at all, and without them there would be no way to navigate within a site, or to direct people to external sites. A website would be nothing more than a single page!

THE ANCHOR ELEMENT

At the heart of the hyperlink mechanism lies the anchor element, < a >. It is called this because one of its uses is for marking specific points in a page. This use remains, but < a > is most commonly used for creating hyperlinks.

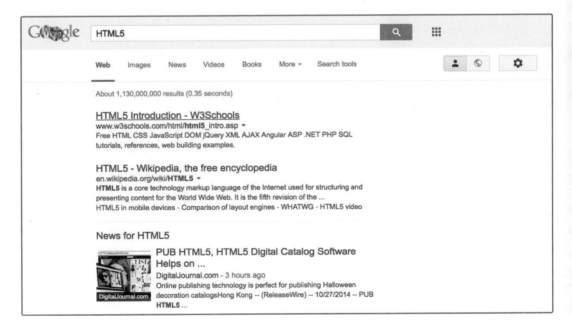

Above: Without hyperlinks there'd be no such thing as Google.

```
8
9
10    <body>
11
12        <p>HTML5 info can be found on <a href="www.google.com">Google</a>. It's a useful resource.</p>
13
14    </body>
15
16
```

Above: Using an <a> element to create a hyperlink.

Creating a Hyperlink

We create a hyperlink by wrapping an <a> element around the text we want to convert into a hyperlink – the **URL** (or web address) that you want to link to is defined in the href attribute of the <a>.

URLs

URL stands for Uniform Resource Locator. There are two common forms of URL: **absolute** and **relative**. The former defines a full web address for a resource, starting with 'http://'. The latter operates relative to the current file, and can only address resources within the same site as that file. A relative URL states the path from the current page to a resource, along with the resource's filename, and looks like 'pathToFile/filename'.

STYLING LINKS

As with all elements, < a > has a default appearance derived ultimately from the browser's default style sheet. In the case of < a > that default styling is typically for blue underlined text. We can override this, of course, by attaching style rules to an < a > element, either directly or via style inheritance.

However, a hyperlink typically changes styling depending upon its state, i.e. if the mouse pointer is over it, if the user has previously clicked the link, etc. This state-based styling is achieved through CSS **Pseudo-Class** selectors.

Hot Tip

A web browser provides a default style sheet. This defines values for all CSS properties, and is the starting point of the style cascade.

Below: Hyperlinks have a default appearance.

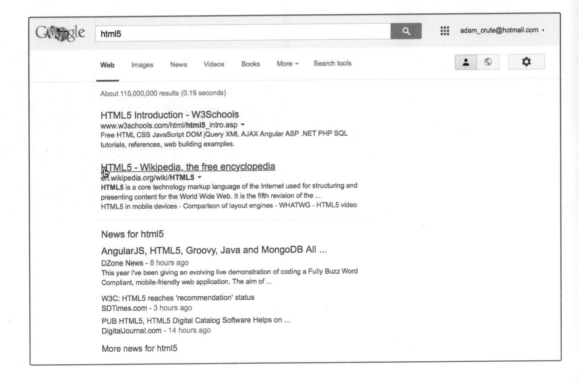

Pseudo-Class Selectors

A pseudo-class is a class that's not specifically declared in an HTML document, but that becomes available when the page is being viewed in a browser. There are a few different ones, but with hyperlinks the pseudo-classes we're concerned with are :link (the base-state of a hyperlink), :hover (the mouse pointer is over the hyperlink) and :visited (the hyperlink has been clicked). In CSS we use these pseudo-class selectors as a suffix to another selector.

```
1
2   a:link {
3        color:blue;
4   }
5
6   a:hover {
7        color:red;
8        text-decoration:none;
9   }
10
11  a:visited {
12       color:purple;
13  }
14
15  .navButton:hover {
16       colour:blue;
17       background-color:gray;
18       cursor:pointer;
19  }
20
21  #headerLogo:hover {
22       border-color:blue;
23       border-style:solid;
24       border-width:2px;
25       cursor:pointer;
26  }
```

Above: Pseudo-Class selectors are added as a suffix to another selector.

OPENING A HYPERLINK IN A NEW WINDOW

It's often desirable to open a hyperlink in a new browser window so your own site remains open in the background. This is done via the target attribute of the <a> element, like so:

```
<a href="http://www.bbc.co.uk" target="_blank">
```

LISTS

Lists are a staple part of web design. There are two basic list types, unordered and ordered, both of which will contain one or more list items. A third type, the definition list, creates a glossary-like structure of titles and associated information.

LIST ITEMS

Before looking at the list elements themselves, let's consider what goes into a list. In HTML this is a **list item** element, `<li>`. Typically, these contain text but, as with other text-based elements, can also contain other elements such as images and hyperlinks. <li> elements are rendered in the order in which they appear in the parent list element.

Above: Lists allow us to present information in an attractive and logical manner.

Unordered List

- HTML5 is largely made up of elements.
- Elements are demarked by opening and closing tags.
- Attributes allow you to modify an element.

Ordered List

1. HTML5 is largely made up of elements.
2. Elements are demarked by opening and closing tags.
3. Attributes allow you to modify an element.

Definition List

HTML5
    is largely made up of elements.
Elements
    are demarked by opening and closing tags
Attributes
    allow you to modify an element.

UNORDERED LISTS

An unordered list, `<ul>`, is a simple bullet-point list. Each `<li>` added to the list creates a new bullet-point. The `list-style-type` and `list-style-image` style properties determine the appearance of the bullet-point markers.

```
13
14              ul {
15                  list-style-type:circle;
16              }
17
18              ol {
19 ▾                list-style-type:decimal;
20              }                        ⬥ armenian
21          </style>                     ⬥ circle
22      </head>                          ⬥ cjk-ideographic
23                                       ⬥ decimal
24      <body>                           ⬥ decimal-leading-zero
25                                       ⬥ disc
26          <h2>Unordered List</h2>      ⬥ georgian
27          <ul>                         ⬥ hebrew
28              <li>HTML5 is largely made up of elements.</li>  ⬥ hiragana
29              <li>Elements are demarked by opening and closing tags.</li>  ⬥ hiragana-iroha
30              <li>Attributes allow you to modify an element.</li>
31          </ul>
32
33          <h2>Ordered List</h2>
34          <ol>
35              <li>HTML5 is largely made up of elements.</li>
36              <li>Elements are demarked by opening and closing tags.</li>
37              <li>Attributes allow you to modify an element.</li>
38          </ol>
39
40      </body>
41
```

Above: `<ul>` and `<ol>` lists only differ in the way each item is marked.

ORDERED LISTS

In an ordered list, `<ol>`, each item is marked with a sequential number or letter. Interestingly, the style of numbering is determined by the `list-style-type` style property, the same as with a `<ul>`. This shows that the only real difference between `<ul>` and `<ol>` is the styling!

DEFINITION LISTS

A definition list, `<dl>`, is a bit like a glossary: each item consists of a title and a block of information relating to the title. This means that each item in the list actually has two components: a `<dt>` element for the title and a `<dd>` element for the information (the second 'd' representing the word 'data').

```
19    <body>
20
21        <h2>Definition List</h2>
22        <dl>
23            <dt>HTML5</dt>
24            <dd>is largely made up of elements.</dd>
25            <dt>Elements</dt>
26            <dd>are demarked by opening and closing tags</dd>
27            <dt>Attributes</dt>
28            <dd>allow you to modify an element.</dd>
29        </dl>
30
31    </body>
32
```

Definition List

HTML5
   is largely made up of elements.
Elements
   are demarked by opening and closing tags
Attributes
   allow you to modify an element.

Above: Each item in a `<dl>` comprises two elements: `<dt>` and `<dd>`.

LISTS WITHIN LISTS

If you wish to create a multi-tiered list, the solution is to place a new list element within an `<li>` or `<dd>` element. You can do this with any of the three list types, and you can mix and match the different types as required.

CREATING WEBSITES

BUILDING A WEBSITE

The process of building a website is much more than just adding HTML and CSS. Here we show how to plan a site, build it with HTML and CSS, and how to get a website online.

PLANNING AND SKETCHING

When building a web page it's not simply a matter of jumping straight in and starting to code with HTML and CSS. Any good website will need some planning. This helps to determine the layout and where the various page elements are to be placed, in turn helping to speed up the design and development process.

What Should a Sketch Include?

A sketch could be as simple as a few boxes showing the main layout elements and a few additional details. However, the more details and thought put into a sketch, the easier the build

Below: Get a browser sketchpad to plan your site.

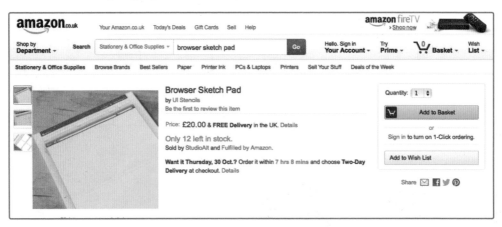

will be further down the line. For example, additional sketches could be made for specific elements of the site such as the `<header>`.

CREATE A WIREFRAME

Once a final sketch (or sketches) has been completed the next step is to create a wireframe. This is not essential, but is another useful part of the planning process. A wireframe is a more precise version of a sketch, which helps determine the layout. Try out https://wireframe.cc/ for quick and simple wireframe creation.

Below: Creating a wireframe helps envisage a page layout.

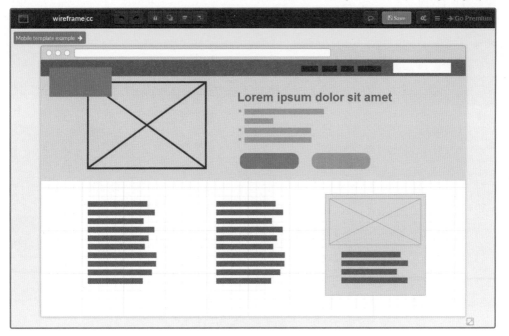

TOOLS OF THE TRADE

You cannot build a website without the right tools. The basic set-up includes a text editor and an image editor. The text editor will be where the HTML and CSS is created, while the image editor will allow for the manipulation and modification of images and graphics.

Hot Tip

If you are using TextEdit on a Mac, be sure to switch to plain text mode before you start coding: [shift]+[cmd]+[T].

TEXT EDITORS

Windows and MacOSX both come with text editors: Notepad and TextEdit respectively. These are ideal for beginners, but are very basic. There are some free editors worth checking out. Try Notepad++ (http://notepad-plus-plus.org); Brackets (http://brackets.io); CoffeeCup Free HTML Editor (http://www.coffeecup.com/free-editor/) or the more advanced Sublime Text (http://www.sublimetext.com)

TopStyle 5, a powerful HTML5 & CSS3 editor for Windows.

What makes TopStyle 5 special
What's new in TopStyle 5?
Download and try it free!

Above: Try different text editors to see which one works for you.

HTML EDITORS

HTML editors provide lots of features for the web developer. The best known is Adobe Dreamweaver; it is excellent but is expensive and can only be licensed on a subscription basis. HTML editors offer features such as code-hinting and code-colouring, both of which are invaluable to the developer.

```
 3   <html>
 4
 5       <head>
 6           <!--TO DO: Come up with a better title for the page -->
 7           <title>My Page</title>
 8           <link rel="stylesheet" type="text/css" href="siteStyles.css"/>
 9           <style>
10               body {
11                   font-family:Arial, Helvetica, sans-serif;
12                   font-size:14px;
13                   color:black;
14                   padd:
15               }              padding
16           </style>          padding-bottom
17       </head>               padding-left
18                             padding-right
19       <body>                padding-top
20           <header>
21               <h1>A Page All About Me</h1>
22           </header>
23
24           <section>
25               <h2>What I'm thinking now</h2>
26               <!-- Placeholder text...-->
27               <p>Lorem ipsum dolor sit amet, consectetuer adipiscing <a href="contactPage.html">elit</a>.
Sed sagittis ante malesuada velit. Curabitur suscipit. Suspendisse quis nibh aliquam sem pulvinar
sollicitudin. Etiam venenatis. Curabitur luctus.</p>
28           </section>
29
```

Code-hinting saves you from having to remember every element and style property name.

Code-colouring helps the developer recognize types of code. Notice how elements, attributes, CSS, comments and plain text content are all easily distinguishable.

Line numbering helps you to know where you are in the document especially if you need to move back and forth through the document.

IMAGE EDITORS

You will often find yourself needing to edit images and create graphics for your site. The professional choice is a combination of Adobe's Photoshop and Illustrator, but this is an expensive route to take with a steep learning curve.

Image and Graphics Editor Links

- **PaintShop Pro (Win):** www.paintshoppro.com
- **CorelDRAW (Win):** www.coreldraw.com
- **Pixelmator (Mac):** www.pixelmator.com
- **iDraw (Mac):** www.indeeo.com
- **Adobe Photoshop (Win/Mac):** www.adobe.com
- **Adobe Illustrator (Win/Mac):** www.adobe.com

BUILDING A WEB PAGE

We've covered a lot of theory and information over the preceding chapters, so let's start putting it into practice. The first step is to create an HTML document and add the basic structure of elements that we're going to use.

CREATE A WORKING FOLDER

The first thing to do is to create a folder in which to store all of the files for our page. Your Documents folder would be a good place for this or, better still, create a folder called MySites inside your Home folder; this can then be a central location for all of the sites you develop. Wherever you put it, the folder you create for an individual site should have the same name as the site. Let's call this one MyFirstSite.

Hot Tip

Don't use spaces in file or folder names. Either remove the spaces and capitalize each word (known as CamelCase), or replace the spaces with underscores or hyphens.

Above: All files for a site should be stored in a single outer folder. It's also handy to place all of your sites into a single outer folder.

Create a Basic Structure

1. Create a new page in your editor of choice and add the DOCTYPE declaration at the very top of the page.

```
1  <!DOCTYPE HTML>
2
3  <html>
4
5      <head>
6
7      </head>
8
9      <body>
10
11     </body>
12
```

Step 2: Start with the essential elements.

2. Add the base elements `<html>`, `<head>` and `<body>`, and save the page as 'index.html' inside your MyFirstSite folder.

```
1  <!DOCTYPE HTML>
2
3  <html>
4
5      <head>
6          <title>My First Web Page</title>
7      </head>
8
9      <body>
10
11     </body>
12
13 </html>
14
```

Step 3: Choose a title for your page wisely; it can make the difference between the page getting visitors or not.

3. Now add a `<title>` element as a child of (i.e. within) the `<head>` element. Make the title relevant as this will show up in search-engine listings.

4. Now we'll create the basic layout structure for the visible content of the page. Add `<header>`, `<section>` and `<footer>` elements as children of the `<body>` element.

Hot Tip

The default page of any website – the one that is loaded if no specific page is requested – is most often called index.html. There are other names that work, but this one is best.

```
1  <!DOCTYPE HTML>
2
3  <html>
4
5      <head>
6          <title>My First Web Page</title>
7      </head>
8
9      <body>
10
11         <header>
12         </header>
13
14         <section>
15         </section>
16
17         <footer>
18         </footer>
19
20     </body>
21
22 </html>
23
```

Step 4: Add the elements that make up the basic page structure.

```
1  <!DOCTYPE HTML>
2
3  <html>
4
5      <head>
6          <title>My First Web Page</title>
7      </head>
8
9      <body>
10
11         <header>
12             <nav>Home | About | Contact </nav>
13         </header>
14
15         <section>
16         </section>
17
18         <footer>
19         </footer>
20
21     </body>
22
```

Step 5: Create a <nav> element inside the <header>.

```
1  <!DOCTYPE HTML>
2
3  <html>
4
5      <head>
6          <title>My First Web Page</title>
7      </head>
8
9      <body>
10
11         <header>
12             <nav>Home | About | Contact </nav>
13             <hgroup>
14                 <h1>My First Web Page</h1>
15                 <h2>It may be basic, but it rocks</h2>
16             </hgroup>
17         </header>
18
19         <section>
20         </section>
21
22         <footer>
23         </footer>
24
25     </body>
26
```

Step 6: Place the heading elements inside the <header>, and then add some suitable text.

5.   We need a means of navigating our site, so add a <nav> element as the first child of the <header>, and enter some titles for pages you're likely to include in your site.

6.   Now we are going to add some text headings to the <header> element of the page. These headings will be related, so we'll create them inside an <hgroup> element.

7.   The main content of the page is going to be placed inside the <section> element. In the next chapter we're going to add an image that represents the site's content (see page 89), but for now we'll keep to just text.

```
16                  </hgroup>
17              </header>
18
19          <section>
20              <h2>Welcome To My World!</h2>
21              <p>Lorem ipsum dolor sit amet, consectetuer adipi
velit. Curabitur suscipit.</p>
22                  <p>Suspendisse quis nibh aliquam sem pulvinar sol
luctus. Nunc venenatis lacus molestie sapien.</p>
23                  <p>Maecenas elementum aliquet velit!</p>
24          </section>
25
26          <footer>
27          </footer>
28
29      </body>
```

Step 8: Add multiple <p> elements to make the text easy to read.

Hot Tip

From the point of view of heading semantics, an <hgroup> makes all headings embedded within it act as a single heading of the type first declared in the <hgroup>.

8. We're going to add some text to accompany the image we'll be adding later. Use an <h2> heading for this because <h1> has been used in our <header>. Then use <p> elements under the <h2> to hold some introductory text.

9. The <aside> element typically contains content that relates to the main content of a page. Add an <aside> after the <section> element, and add some content to it.

```
19          <section>
20              <h2>Welcome To My World!</h2>
21              <p>Lorem ipsum dolor sit amet, consectetuer adipiscing elit. Sed sagittis ante malesuada
velit. Curabitur suscipit.</p>
22              <p>Suspendisse quis nibh aliquam sem pulvinar sollicitudin. Etiam venenatis. Curabitur
luctus. Nunc venenatis lacus molestie sapien.</p>
23              <p>Maecenas elementum aliquet velit!</p>
24          </section>
25
26          <aside>
27              <h3>By the way...</h3>
28              <p>Ut eget mauris sed leo scelerisque lacinia. Nunc arcu magna, mollis id, ornare ac,
pharetra sit amet, purus.</p>
29              <p>Aliquam luctus consectetuer dolor? In placerat, diam et suscipit posuere, lacus orci
vestibulum libero, vulputate faucibus felis leo sit amet elit: Sed hendrerit felis non urna.</p>
30          </aside>
31
32          <footer>
33          </footer>
```

Step 9: Add a <h3> element followed by a few <p> elements. Place them all within an <aside> element.

10. Finally, we'll add some content to the `<footer>`. This can be information such as contact details, address and copyright information.

```
27              <h3>By the way...</h3>
28              <p>Ut eget mauris sed leo scelerisque lacinia. Nunc arcu magna, mollis id,
29              <p>Aliquam luctus consectetuer dolor? In placerat, diam et suscipit posuer
30          </aside>
31
32          <footer>
33              <p>Donec interdum dui at est. Pellentesque sit amet urna</p>
34              <p>(C) J. Smith, 2014</p>
35              <p><a href="mailto:jsmith789@somehost.com">jsmith789@somehost.com</a></p>
36          </footer>
37
38      </body>
```

Step 10: Make sure the info in your `<footer>` is useful.

11. To complete the `<footer>`, add the same navigation menu that we used at the top of the page; simply copy the whole `<nav>` element and paste it as the last child of the <footer> element.

```
26          <aside>
27              <h3>By the way...</h3>
28              <p>Ut eget mauris sed leo scelerisque lacinia. Nunc arcu magna, mollis id,
29              <p>Aliquam luctus consectetuer dolor? In placerat, diam et suscipit posuer
30          </aside>
31
32          <footer>
33              <p>Donec interdum dui at est. Pellentesque sit amet urna</p>
34              <p>(C) J. Smith, 2014</p>
35              <p><a href="mailto:jsmith789@somehost.com">jsmith789@somehost.com</a></p>
36              <nav>Home | About | Contact </nav>
37          </footer>
38
39      </body>
40
41  </html>
42
43
44
```

Step 11: Adding a navigation menu to the bottom of the screen can prove useful.

12. Save your work. Now find the file on your computer and launch it in your web browser to take a look. Rather basic perhaps, but we haven't cracked out the CSS yet...

Step 12: It may be basic, but it's all your own work. Well done.

STYLING A PAGE WITH CSS

The HTML for our page is now in place but it looks fairly basic as things stand. Let's deal with that now by adding some CSS styling to the page.

EMBEDDED OR EXTERNAL?

The first choice is whether to add the CSS as an embedded or external style sheet. Given that our site only has a single page (for now at least) we'll use an embedded sheet so that all of the code for the page is in one location.

Creating the CSS Code

1. Open index.html in your editor if it isn't already open, and then add a `<style>` element inside the `<head>`.

```
1  <!DOCTYPE HTML>
2
3  <html>
4
5      <head>
6          <title>My First Web Page</title>
7          <style>
8          </style>
9      </head>
10
11     <body>
12
```

Step 1: Add an embedded style sheet in the `<head>` of the page.

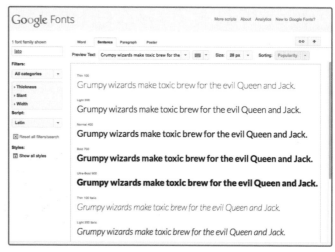

Step 2: Choose a font to use on your website.

Hot Tip

Web fonts allow you to use fonts on your site that aren't installed on your visitors' computers.

2. Now we need a font for our text. There is a limited set of web standard fonts that are installed on all computers; using one of these is an option. The better option is to use a web font: head over to Google Fonts (www.google.com/fonts) and find a font you like, preferably one with a lot of variations, such a Lato.

3. Click the Quick-Use button and select a font variation. You will now be shown a block of code for a `<link>` element. Copy it and paste it into the `<head>` of your page, before the `<style>` element.

Step 3: Copy the `<link>` element code from Google Fonts.

Standard   @import   Javascript

3. Add this code to your website:

```
<link href='http://fonts.googleapis.com/css?family=Lato:400,700,400italic' rel='styleshe
```

```
3   <html>
4
5       <head>
6           <title>My First Web Page</title>
7           <link rel='stylesheet' type='text/css' href='http://fonts.googleapis.com/css?family=Lato:400,700,400italic'/>
8           <style>
9               body {
10                  font-family:"Lato";
11              }
12          </style>
13      </head>
14
15      <body>
16
17          <div id="wrapper">|
18              <header>
19                  <nav>Home | About | Contact </nav>
20                  <hgroup>
21                      <h1>My First Web Page</h1>
22                      <h2>It may be basic, but it rocks</h2>
23                  </hgroup>
24              </header>
25
26              <section>
```

Steps 4 and 5: Use the `font-family` style property to define a font within a style rule, and wrap the page's content in a `<div>`.

4. To make this the default font for the entire page we create a `body` Type selector and set the `font-family` property within its style rule.

5. In order to be able to centralize the page's content area within the browser window, we're going to wrap all of that content in a `<div>` element. Assign an `id` attribute value of `"wrapper"` to the `<div>`.

```
8           <style>
9
10              body {
11                  font-family:"Lato";
12                  font-size:14px;
13              }
14
15              #wrapper {
16                  width:1000px;
17                  height:auto;
18                  margin-left:auto;
19                  margin-right:auto;
20              }
21
22          </style>
23
```

6. We can now style the wrapper `<div>` by using a CSS ID selector of `#wrapper`. Add the code in the screenshot to make the site 1000 pixels wide and centred in the browser window.

Step 6: Styling the wrapper allows it to be centralized in the browser window.

```
8          <style>
9
10             body {
11                 font-family:"Lato";
12                 font-size:14px;
13             }
14
15             #wrapper {
16                 width:1000px;
17                 height:auto;
18                 margin-left:auto;
19                 margin-right:auto;
20             }
21
22             section {
23                 width:700px;
24                 height:auto;
25                 float:left;
26             }
27
28         </style>
29
```

```
11                 font-size:14px;
12             }
13
14             #wrapper {
15                 width:1000px;
16                 height:auto;
17                 margin-left:auto;
18                 margin-right:auto;
19             }
20
21             section {
22                 width:700px;
23                 height:auto;
24                 float:left;
25             }
26
27             aside {
28                 width:300px;
29                 float:right;
30             }
31
32         </style>
```

Step 7: Content within the wrapper now positions itself relative to the wrapper rather than the browser window.

7. The `<section>` element in our page contains the main page content. Copy the CSS code in the screenshot to make it 700 pixels wide and positioned to the left of the wrapper.

Hot Tip

Try using more than one font on a website: one for headings, and one for paragraph text. Best practice is to use no more than three fonts on a page.

8. Now we'll make the `<aside>` element 300 pixels wide and make it float to the left of the `<section>` element. The widths of section and aside will now add up to the 1000 pixel width of the wrapper `<div>`.

Step 8: Floating is a method of positioning one element alongside another.

Step 9: Size the `<footer>` to be the same width as the content above it – this ensures it will float below that content.

```
22              section {
23                  width:700px;
24                  height:auto;
25                  float:left;
26              }
27
28              aside {
29                  width:300px;
30                  float:right;
31              }
32
33              footer {
34                  width:1000px;
35                  height:auto;
36                  float:left;
37              }
```

Step 10: Style heading elements such that they have reducing levels of visual prominence.

```
40              h1 {
41                  font-weight:bold;
42                  font-size:26px;
43                  color:#990000;
44              }
45
46              h2 {
47                  font-weight:bold;
48                  font-size:22px;
49                  color:#CC6600;
50              }
51
52              h3 {
53                  font-weight:normal;
54                  font-size:18px;
55                  font-style:italic;
56                  color:#FF9933;
57              }
58
59              hgroup > h1 {
60                  margin-bottom:3px;
61              }
62
63              hgroup > h2 {
64                  margin-top:0px;
65              }
66
67          </style>
```

9. The `<footer>` sits directly below the text in the `<aside>`. This needs to be styled, again by using float and setting the width to 1000 pixels, the same width as the wrapper `<div>`.

10. Next we'll apply some styling to the heading text, making them different sizes and colours. Experiment until you're happy with the results.

11. A `<footer>` tends to be separated from the main content of a page. This can be done by making it a different colour or by adding a border to the top of the `<footer>`.

Hot Tip

Keep the width of a page to a maximum of 1280 pixels to make sure that the site will look good on the vast majority of desktop screens.

GETTING ONLINE

It's no good going to all that effort to build a website and then keeping it hidden away on your computer – it needs to be out there on the web! To do this you need a domain name, a web server and an FTP Client application for managing your site's files.

DOMAIN NAME

A domain name is the human-readable name that is associated with the IP address of your website, for example, Google's domain name is google.com. This is a unique name that needs **registering** so that it is assigned to you. To do this you use a domain name **registrar** such as 1&1 (www.1and1.co.uk) or 123-reg (www.123-reg.co.uk).

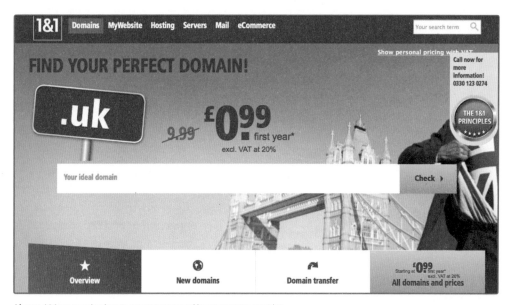

Above: 1&1 is a popular domain name registrar and hosting service provider.

WEB SERVER

Your website needs to be available on the internet, and for this you need a web server. The easiest way to get one is via a web-hosting service; this provides you with your own web server. ISPs often include such services as part of your rental package. Alternatively you can buy hosting services for a little as £1/month from the likes of 1&1 and 123-reg.

TRANSFERRING FILES

FTP (File Transfer Protocol) provides a means for transferring files across a network, and is the best method for getting your site files onto your web server. There are numerous FTP Client applications, with Filezilla (http://filezilla-project.org) and CyberDuck (http://cyberduck.io) being popular choices on Windows and Mac respectively.

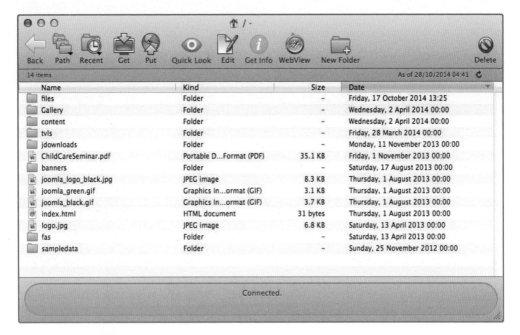

Above: An FTP Client application allows you to transfer files to and from your web server.

ADDING A BLOG TO YOUR SITE

Web logs, or blogs to give them their usual name, are a common addition to a website, and help you build a community of users with similar interests to you.

TWO EASY OPTIONS

From a programing point of view, blogs are quite complex; you've come a long way, but you're not ready to tackle that particular project just yet! Thankfully, then, you can add a blog to your site without having to build your own, and your newly acquired knowledge of HTML and CSS can be brought to bear on customizing the blog. You can either link from your site to an external blog provider, or install third-party blogging software on your web server. WordPress is a great option for both scenarios.

Below: Sign up for a free WordPress site at www.wordpress.com.

Wordpress.com

Despite having grown into a complete **CMS** (Content Management System), WordPress is, at its core, a blogging system and can still be used as such. If you wish to keep things as simple as possible then head along to www.wordpress.com and create a site with them. Follow the excellent tutorials on the site to get your blog up and running, and then link to it from your regular website.

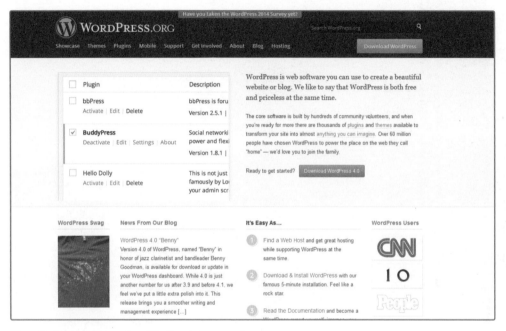

Above: The latest installable version of WordPress is at www.wordpress.org.

Wordpress.org

You can also install WordPress on your own website. Often it is provided as an option by your web server host; all you need to do is switch it on from your server control panel. Alternatively, the software can also be downloaded from www.wordpress.org if it's not offered pre-installed by your host. You can then use WordPress to create blog pages or, indeed, to run your entire site. Full documentation is available from www.wordpress.org.

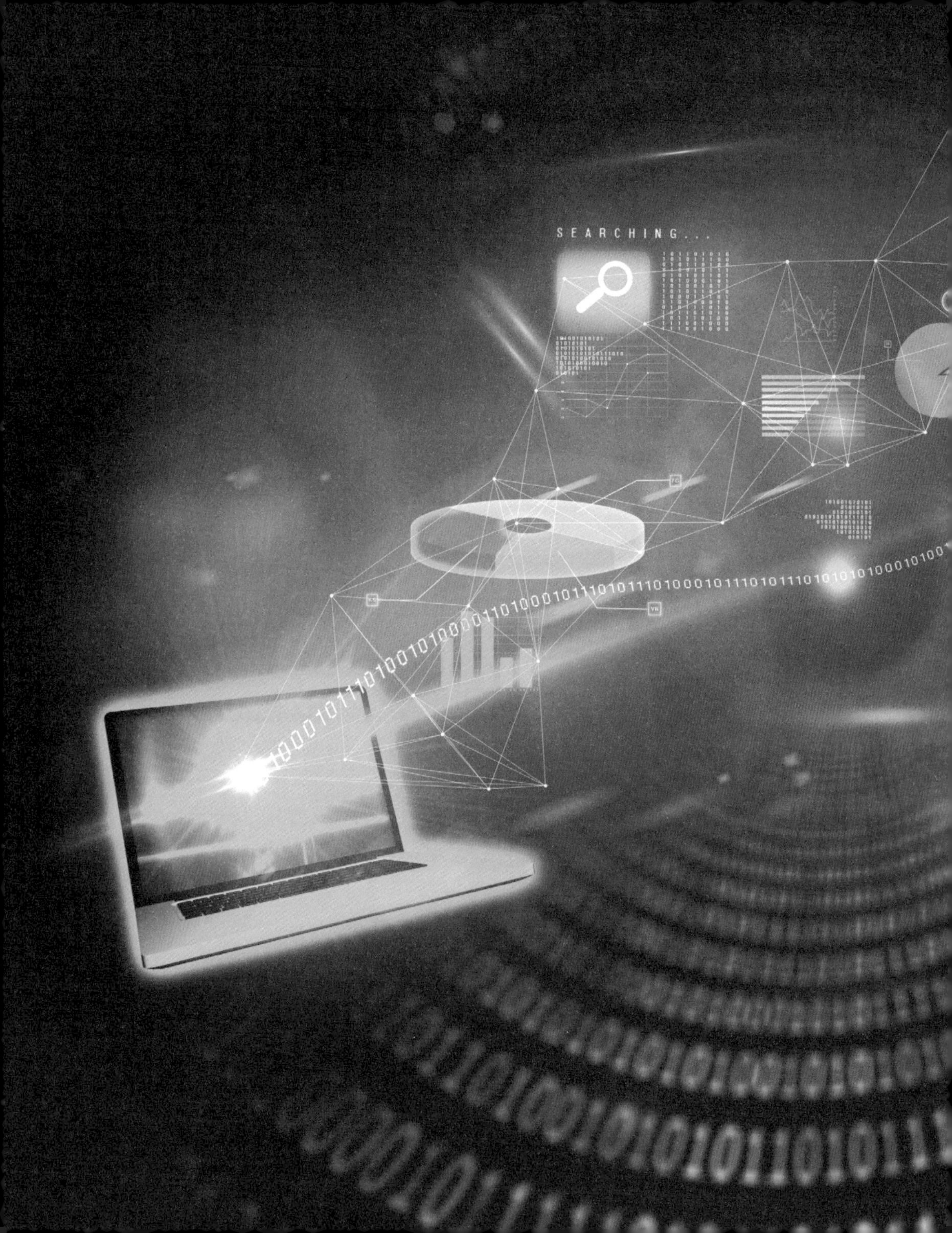
SEARCHING...

IMAGES, VIDEO &
OTHER ENHANCEMENTS

ADDING MEDIA TO YOUR WEBSITE

Most websites contain a lot more than just text. Images, video and audio can greatly increase your visitor numbers and encourage them to stay longer. Advanced HTML5 features such as geolocation can improve your site's interactions with your visitors and, of course, adding a sprinkle of visual polish is always a good idea.

WORKING WITH IMAGES

Alongside text, images are the element that almost every website has in common. Very rarely will you find a contemporary website with a total lack of imagery. Images are extremely versatile and have the potential to make a website much more visually appealing.

Above: Caption to go here. Caption to go here. Caption to go here. Caption to go here. Caption to go here. Caption to go

IMAGE FORMATS

Images come in a variety of formats, but on the web there are effectively three formats used: GIF, PNG and JPG. The GIF format is a hangover from the early days of the web and is becoming increasingly uncommon. PNG and JPG, on the other hand, are widely used. Both have specific advantages and disadvantages, but together they can satisfy all situations.

The PNG Format

PNG (Portable Network Graphics, pronounced 'ping') is the best option for graphics (as opposed to photo-based imagery) because typically they use lossless compression and so offer better sharpness and accuracy than JPG. Their other benefit is that they support transparency. This means that a PNG image needn't have a solid-coloured background, and that anything behind them can show through the transparent areas of the PNG.

Below: The PNG image format is often the best for small graphic elements like logos.

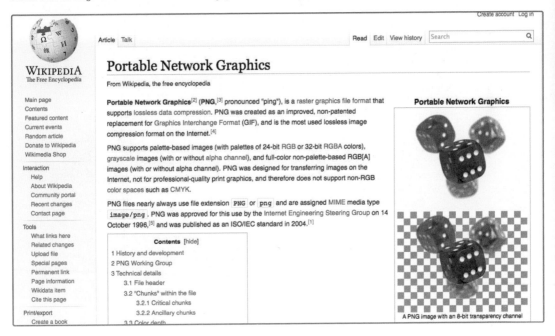

The JPG Format

The JPG format (also known as JPEG, pronounced 'jay-peg') uses a complex image compression technique to reduce the file size of an image without visibly degrading it. This means that the images can be saved at different quality levels to reduce the file size of an image. The higher the level, the better the quality, but the larger the file size; the developer can choose where to strike the balance. JPGs don't support transparency and so are not as suitable for graphics.

Hot Tip

When creating images and graphics, work from a full quality editable version in a lossless format such as PSD (Photoshop's native format), then export the graphics you need as PNG or JPG files.

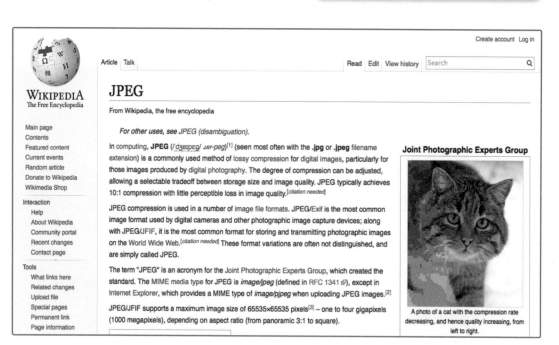

Above: Photos are usually saved in the JPG format.

ADDING IMAGES

The addition of images to a web page is a relatively simple process. However, before adding an image, it is a good idea to store your images in a sub-folder of your site root.

THE <IMG> ELEMENT

When adding images to a page we use the <img> element. This is a self-closing element, meaning that, you will recall, they only have an opening tag and no closing tag, and can't have any content nested within them.

How to Add an Image

1. In the previous chapter we built a simple page in a folder called MyFirstSite. Locate this folder and create a subfolder within it; name the subfolder 'images'.

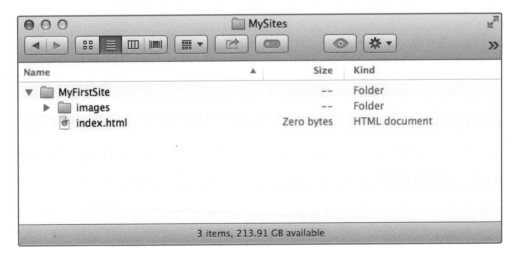

Step 1: Make sure the 'images' folder is a subfolder of the site root folder.

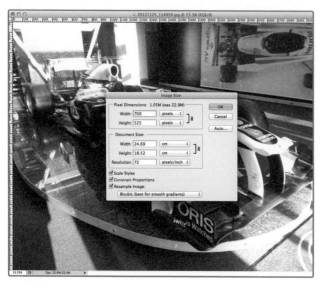

Step 2: Image editors can resize an image whilst retaining the correct proportions.

2. Find a suitable image. Use your image editor to resize it to 700 pixels wide and whatever height is proportional to that width for your chosen image. Save a copy of the image into the folder we have just created, using the JPG format. Name the file homepageImage.jpg.

3. Open your site's homepage (index. html) in your text or HTML editor, and locate the <h2> element that's at the top of the <section> element. Create an empty line in the HTML, above the <h2> element.

```
74
75      <body>
76
77          <div id="wrapper">
78              <header>
79                  <nav>Home | About | Contact </nav>
80                  <hgroup>
81                      <h1>My First Web Page</h1>
82                      <h2>It may be basic, but it rocks</h2>
83                  </hgroup>
84              </header>
85
86          <section>
87              |
88                  <h2>Welcome To My World!</h2>
89                  <p>Lorem ipsum dolor sit amet, consectetuer adipiscing elit. Sed sagittis ante malesuada
velit. Curabitur suscipit.</p>
90                  <p>Suspendisse quis nibh aliquam sem pulvinar sollicitudin. Etiam venenatis. Curabitur
luctus. Nunc venenatis lacus molestie sapien. Phasellus erat. Vestibulum posuere varius dolor. Aenean id
arcu. Sed mauris mauris, consectetuer nec, accumsan ut.</p>
91                  <p>Maecenas elementum aliquet velit!</p>
92          </section>
```

Step 3: Create an empty line in the HTML code.

```
79              <nav>Home I About I Contact </nav>
80              <hgroup>
81                  <h1>My First Web Page</h1>
82                  <h2>It may be basic, but it rocks</h2>
83              </hgroup>
84          </header>
85
86          <section>
87              <img id="homepageImage"
88                  name="Williams"
89                  alt="What a day at the Williams factory!"
90                  src="images/homepageImage.jpg"
91              />
92              <h2>Welcome To My World!</h2>
93              <p>Lorem ipsum dolor sit amet, consectetuer adipiscing elit. Sed sagittis ante malesuada
    velit. Curabitur suscipit.</p>
94                  <p>Suspendisse quis nibh aliquam sem pulvinar sollicitudin. Etiam venenatis. Curabitur
    luctus. Nunc venenatis lacus molestie sapien. Phasellus erat. Vestibulum posuere varius dolor. Aenean id
    arcu. Sed mauris mauris, consectetuer nec, accumsan ut.</p>
95                  <p>Maecenas elementum aliquet velit!</p>
96          </section>
97
```

Step 4: When defining more than a couple of attributes, it's not unusual to split them into separate indented lines, making them easier to read.

4. Now add the <img> element as shown in the illustration. The name attribute value will be displayed in place of the image if the browser is unable to load it, whilst the alt attribute value is the text that is shown if the user hovers the mouse pointer above the image. The src attribute value is the URL of the image to use (note we're using a relative URL).

5. We're going to create a style rule for the image, so find the <style> element in the <head> of your page. Add the code shown in the illustration. Note that we're using an ID selector so that we target only our newly added <img> element. Save your work and be sure to view the results in your web browser.

```
54
55          h3 {
56              font-weight:normal;
57              font-size:18px;
58              font-style:italic;
59              color:#FF9933;
60          }
61
62          hgroup > h1 {
63              margin-bottom:3px;
64          }
65
66          hgroup > h2 {
67              margin-top:0px;
68              margin-bottom:0px;
69          }
70
71          #homepageImage {
72              float:left;
73              border-style:none;
74          }
75
76      </style>
77
```

Step 5: Some browsers draw a border around an image; use the border-style property to control this behaviour.

ADDING VIDEO

Video is a medium that is very commonplace in web pages and websites. They are attention-grabbing and are much more engaging than a static image. Users want to watch video, and a ten-second video clip can impart far more information than an image and text occupying the same space.

VIDEO OPTIONS

There are two main options for adding video to a web page. One is to use the `<video>` element, while the other (and simpler) option is to embed a YouTube (or similar) video into a page. In basic setups, the `<video>` element requires the actual video file to be stored on your web server. Embedding a YouTube video is simply a matter of copying and pasting code provided by YouTube.

```
1  <!DOCTYPE HTML>
2
3  <html>
4
5      <head>
6          <title>My Video Page</title>
7      </head>
8
9      <body>
10
11          <video src="videos/stoneham.mp4"></video>
12
13      </body>
14
15  </html>
16
```

Above: Adding video to a site used to be difficult; with HTML5 it's a doddle.

ADD A VIDEO WITH HTML

To embed a video into a page, add a `<video>` element to its HTML. There are two ways to specify the video file that's to be played. The simplest is to use the `<video>` element's `src`

attribute, into which the video's URL is entered. However, due to the fact that different browsers support different formats of video, it's not uncommon to provide multiple versions of the video in different file formats. When doing this we have to embed a `<source>` element within the `<video>` element for each file format you provide.

Hot Tip

If hosting your own videos, favour the MP4 file format. You should also consider including a version in Ogg-Theora format to improve browser and OS compatibility (http://theora.org).

```
1   <!DOCTYPE HTML>
2
3   <html>
4
5       <head>
6           <title>My Video Page</title>
7       </head>
8
9       <body>
10
11          <video>
12              <source src="videos/stoneham.mp4" type="video/mp4">
13              <source src="videos/stoneham.ogv" type="video/ogg">
14          </video>
15
16      </body>
17
18  </html>
19
```

Above: The `<source>` element allows you to include multiple versions of a video.

Above: Embedding a YouTube video is simply a copy and paste job.

ADD A YOUTUBE VIDEO

Adding a YouTube video is much simpler than hosting your own. If it's a video you've produced yourself then you will need a Google account to allow you to upload the material to YouTube. Once there, though, hooking your video into your page couldn't be easier.

The <iframe> Element

All videos on YouTube have a button underneath them marked Share. Clicking this button reveals a panel with three tabs along the top and a field containing some code. Clicking the Embed tab will generate the HTML code for an <iframe>, an element that creates a portal between your site and another. Copy the <iframe> code and paste it into your page's HTML: simple!

ADDING AUDIO

HTML5's new `<audio>` element works on very much the same principle as `<video>`. As with `<video>`, the `<audio>` element supports multiple source files in order to improve browser and OS compatibility.

AUDIO FORMATS

Whilst you may think MP3 audio files are ubiquitous, licensing considerations mean they are not supported in all browsers on all operating systems (it is the same situation with video, as already alluded to). Including your audio content in both MP3 and Ogg-Vorbis formats should cover all the bases, though.

Hot Tip

The Ogg-Vorbis audio format is partner to the Ogg-Theora video format. Both are open-source software and are therefore free to use. Pop along to http://vorbis.com for information and encoding tools.

```
4
5      <head>
6          <title>My Video Page</title>
7      </head>
8
9      <body>
10
11         <audio src="music/TheSentinel.mp3"></audio>
12
13         <audio>
14             <source src="music/TheSentinel.mp3" type="audio/mp3">
15             <source src="music/TheSentinel.oga" type="audio/ogg">
16         </audio>
17
18     </body>
19
```

Above: Including audio content in a page is a doddle with the `<audio>` element.

GOING BEYOND THE BASICS

HTML5 and CSS3 represent significant advances in their respective languages. Here we introduce some of the more advanced features of both languages. A full discussion is beyond the scope of this book, but you should be aware of these features.

HTML5 FORMS

A simple example of the power of HTML5 lies in HTML forms. Before HTML5, creating forms for the web typically involved the use of coding with **JavaScript**. For instance, if you wished to verify that the user had entered suitable data into a **form** the only way to do so was via scripting. HTML5 forms, however, have built-in validation features, saving the developer heaps of time and complexity.

Below: HTML5 forms greatly simplify validation of user entries.

Email Sign-up Form Demo

I've created a demo of an email sign-up form you can check out at http://richardshepherd.com /tv/forms/.

html5 forms demo

First Name
Richard

HTML5 DRAG-AND-DROP

Drag-and-drop is fundamental to computer use, and is a very intuitive way for a user to interact with on-screen objects. In HTML5, adding the `draggable` attribute to any visual element and setting the attribute's value to `"true"` makes that element draggable: `<img id="#homepageImage" draggable="true" />`. Handling such interactions remains the job of a scripting language like JavaScript.

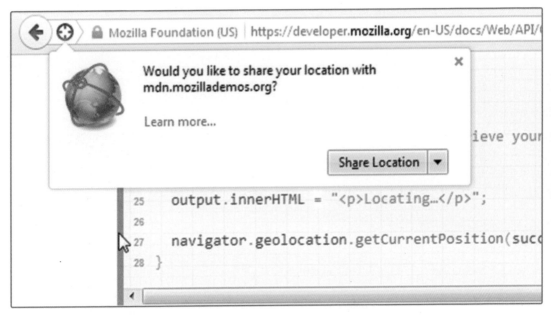

Above: The user will be asked whether or not they wish to share their geolocation data with your site.

HTML5 GEOLOCATION

The HTML5 geolocation feature is used to determine a person's location through their desktop or mobile device. A popular use of geolocation is on mobile devices where it integrates with maps. It is used for a host of services that need your location, for example, for getting directions from A to B.

CSS TRANSFORMS

Transforms manipulate the visual appearance of HTML elements. For example, the `rotate` style property will rotate an element. This makes it easy to turn a square into a diamond, for example. Other properties include `scale` and `skew`. The former makes an element larger, whilst the latter tilts an element.

CSS TRANSITIONS

Transitions allow elements to change visually over a specified time period. A simple example of the transition property is typically found on buttons. These will have an initial background colour which fades to another colour when the mouse cursor is hovered over the button. Used subtly, such effects add a touch of class to a site.

```
7
8        <style>
9            div {
10                position:absolute;
11                width:100px;
12                height:100px;
13                background-color:red;
14            }
15
16            #box {
17                left:200px;
18                top:200px;
19            }
20
21            #rotatedBox {
22                left:400px;
23                top:200px;
24                transform:rotate(45deg);
25            }
26        </style>
27
```

Left & Above: Transforms allow the position and orientation of elements to be adjusted.

How Transitions Work

We already know how to use Pseudo-Class selectors to make an <a> element respond to different states, such as :hover, when the mouse pointer is over an element. What you may not realize is that Pseudo-Class selectors can operate on any visual element. This is the key to triggering a transition; we define it within a Pseudo-Class selector's style rule.

For example, if we had an element with an id of "homeButton", then we could target a specific style rule at this button when the mouse is over it using an ID selector. We would then define the transition within the style rule (see illustration).

```
19
20
21     #homeButton:hover {
22         transition-property:background-colour;
23         transition-duration:0.6s;
24         transition-timing-function:ease;
25         background-color:blue;
26     }
27
28
```

Above: There are a number of style properties that, taken together, define the transition.

CSS KEYFRAMES

Keyframes are a concept from the world of animation. They specify a point in time and the state of an object at that point – the intermediate steps between the keyframes can then be calculated by the computer. Until HTML5 and CSS3 came along, Adobe Flash was the standard for creating keyframed animations on a web page, but not any more!

Apply an Animation

Animations can be applied to almost every element in a web page. Here we are going to demonstrate how to animate a `<div>` element moving across the screen.

Hot Tip

Related groups of CSS properties often have a shorthand equivalent that can set all such properties in one line of code. For example, the various animation-style properties can be declared simultaneously via the `animation` **property.**

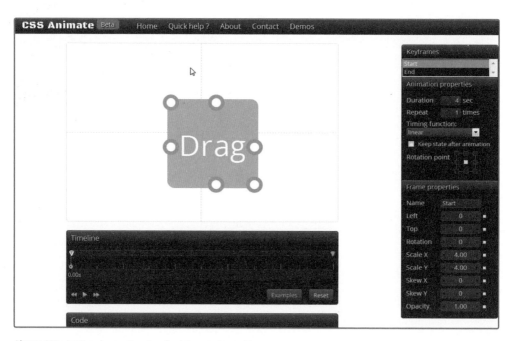

Above: CSS animation changes the value of a style property over time.

Creating a Simple Animation

1. Create a new HTML document, add the basic structural elements (`<html>`, `<head>` and `<body>`) and create a `<style>` element in the `<head>`. Save the file as movingbox.html.

2. Add a `<div>` within the body and give it an id of 'boxToMove'. In the `<style>` element create an ID selector and define a style rule that will size the `<div>` to 100 x 100 pixels and give it a background colour so we can see it on-screen.

3. We'll now add the animation code to the style rule. Copy the style properties and values from the illustration; the style property names are self-explanatory.

```
1   <!DOCTYPE HTML>
2
3   <html>
4
5       <head>
6           <title>CSS Animation</title>
7           <style>
8           </style>
9       </head>
10
11      <body>
12
13      </body>
14
15  </html>
16
```

Step 1: Create a basic document called movingbox.html.

```
7       <style>
8
9           #boxToMove {
10              position:relative;
11              width:100px;
12              height:100px;
13              background-color:red;
14              animation-name:boxMover;
15              animation-duration:3s;
16              animation-iteration-count:infinite;
17          }
18
19
20      </style>
```

Steps 2 & 3: The style rules define both the appearance of the movingbox `<div>`, and its animation properties.

Hot Tip

Not all browsers support keyframe animation – if it's not working for you, try opening the page in Firefox.

4. The final part of the jigsaw is the keyframe code. This is declared in a way we have not yet investigated, using a CSS '@' declaration, in this case @keyframes. This is followed by the name of the animation, the same name as is declared in the animation-name style property.

```
7          <style>
8
9              #boxToMove {
10                 position:relative;
11                 width:100px;
12                 height:100px;
13                 background-color:red;
14                 animation-name:boxMover;
15                 animation-duration:3s;
16                 animation-iteration-count:infinite;
17             }
18
19             @keyframes boxMover {
20                 0%    {top:0px;}
21                 25%   {top:100px;}
22                 75%   {top:50px;}
23                 100%  {top:150px;}
24             }
```

Steps 4 & 5: The code following the @keyframes declaration defines which style properties will be animated, and what values they'll take at various points in time.

5. The lines of code that follow the @keyframes declaration define a style property and value against various points in time, expressed as percentages. The top style property we are using determines the distance between the top of the animated element and the top of its containing block, in this case the <body> element.

6. Save your work and open the file in a browser to see the results.

WHAT IS JAVASCRIPT?

We already know that HTML creates the structure for a page and defines its content, and that CSS controls the visual look of that content. Scripting completes this picture by providing the means to control the behaviour of your page, and how it reacts to user interaction. There are various scripting languages for the web, but the main one – built into all web browsers – is JavaScript.

WHERE DOES JAVASCRIPT FIT?

Earlier we used the analogy of a house to describe HTML and CSS, the former being the bricks and mortar, and the latter being the decoration and finish. If we stick with this analogy, JavaScript (or JS for short) would be a smart-house control system that can control every aspect of the house intricately.

Right: JavaScript is the most common scripting language used in web pages.

Adding a Script

The intricacies of JavaScript are beyond the scope of this book, but there are pre-written scripts available on the internet that you may wish to incorporate into your site; to this end let's see how you add a script to a page.

The <script> Element

Like CSS, a script can be embedded into your page or be external to your page. The latter is the more common approach, but both are achieved via the <script> element: an embedded script is written between the opening and closing <script> tags; an external script is located in a separate text file and is linked to a page using the src attribute of the <script> element.

Below: Like CSS, scripts can be embedded or external.

```
5      <head>
6          <title>Script Elements</title>
7
8          <!--This is an external script...-->
9          <script type="text/javascript" src="js/siteCore.js"></script>
10
11         <!--This is an embedded script...-->|
12         <script type="text/javascript">
13             var com;
14             if(!com) {
15                 com = {};
16             }
17             if(!com.ukmastersdvd) {
18                 com.ukmastersdvd = {};
19             }
20
21             com.ukmastersdvd.resetContactForm = function() {
22                 document.getElementById("messageTitle").setAttribute("value", "");
23                 document.getElementById("messageTitleMessage").textContent = "";
24                 document.getElementById("senderAddress").setAttribute("value", "");
25                 document.getElementById("senderAddressMessage").textContent = "";
26                 document.getElementById("messageBody").textContent = "";
27                 document.getElementById("messageBodyMessage").textContent = "";
28             }
29
30         </script>
31
32     </head>
```

Execute on Sight

A `<script>` element can appear anywhere within a web page, and is executed – in other words, run – when the browser encounters it. Typically, then, scripts that have to be available to the whole page are defined in the `<head>`, whereas scripts that create an output to the page whilst the page is being rendered are positioned at the location that the output is required.

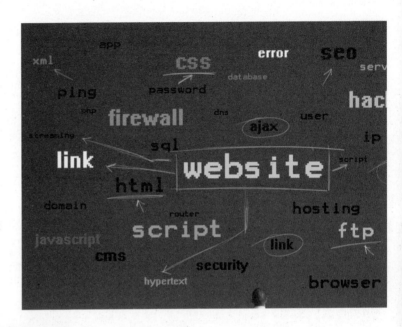

A GOOD UNDERSTANDING

A thorough understanding of JavaScript allows you to take your site well beyond the limitations of HTML and CSS, turning your pages and sites into bona fide web applications, but it's a deep subject with a lot to learn. Many books exist to help you learn JavaScript; the companion to this book, *Coding JavaScript Basics* by Adam Crute, would be an excellent place to start.

Left: *Coding JavaScript Basics* is part of our Everyday Guides Made Easy series, and is the perfect companion to the book you're reading now.

ADVANCED CODING

ADVANCED TEXT

As we have learned, HTML is nothing more than plain text; it only works at all because web browsers recognize characters that have a special meaning in HTML, such as '<' and '>'. But what if we want to use one of those special characters within the text of a page?

SPECIAL CHARACTERS

There are a number of characters that, if typed into a text-based element such as <p>, will cause errors and the page will not be rendered correctly (if at all). For example, we may wish to include angle brackets in a passage about mathematical formulae (or, indeed, HTML), or quote marks when quoting what somebody has said. The problem is that such characters have specific predefined meanings in HTML and so will be misinterpreted by the browser.

Special Characters

"There are many special characters in HTML" said the man. "Characters such as '<' & '>' can't be typed directly into the text of an HTML document." he said.

He went on to explain that the same was true of "extended" characters such as ©, µ and many more. Accented latin characters, such as 'Á' and 'È' are also classed as extended characters, he explained.

Above: Some characters have special meaning in HTML and can't be typed directly into an element.

ASCII and Extended Characters

The core set of character symbols used in computing is referred to as **ASCII** (American Standard Code for Information Interchange, pronounced 'ask-ee'). This is a standard that defines the **character code** used to represent the most common alphabetic, numeric and punctuation characters. There are 128 such character codes, and all computers follow the ASCII standard for these character codes. Characters that fall outside of the ASCII standard, such as accented letters, are known as **extended** characters and shouldn't be typed directly into HTML text.

Right: All computers use the ASCII standard to represent basic letters, numbers and punctuation.

Hot Tip

Internally, computers represent everything with numbers, and this includes text. The number that represents a given alpha-numeric, punctuation or symbol character is called a character code.

ASCII control characters

00	NULL	(Null character)
01	SOH	(Start of Header)
02	STX	(Start of Text)
03	ETX	(End of Text)
04	EOT	(End of Trans.)
05	ENQ	(Enquiry)
06	ACK	(Acknowledgement)
07	BEL	(Bell)
08	BS	(Backspace)
09	HT	(Horizontal Tab)
10	LF	(Line feed)
11	VT	(Vertical Tab)
12	FF	(Form feed)
13	CR	(Carriage return)
14	SO	(Shift Out)
15	SI	(Shift In)
16	DLE	(Data link escape)
17	DC1	(Device control 1)
18	DC2	(Device control 2)
19	DC3	(Device control 3)
20	DC4	(Device control 4)
21	NAK	(Negative acknowl.)
22	SYN	(Synchronous idle)
23	ETB	(End of trans. block)
24	CAN	· (Cancel)
25	EM	(End of medium)
26	SUB	(Substitute)
27	ESC	(Escape)
28	FS	(File separator)
29	GS	(Group separator)
30	RS	(Record separator)
31	US	(Unit separator)
127	DEL	(Delete)

ASCII printable characters

32	space	64	@	96	`
33	!	65	A	97	a
34	"	66	B	98	b
35	#	67	C	99	c
36	$	68	D	100	d
37	%	69	E	101	e
38	&	70	F	102	f
39	'	71	G	103	g
40	(	72	H	104	h
41	)	73	I	105	i
42	*	74	J	106	j
43	+	75	K	107	k
44	,	76	L	108	l
45	-	77	M	109	m
46	.	78	N	110	n
47	/	79	O	111	o
48	0	80	P	112	p
49	1	81	Q	113	q
50	2	82	R	114	r
51	3	83	S	115	s
52	4	84	T	116	t
53	5	85	U	117	u
54	6	86	V	118	v
55	7	87	W	119	w
56	8	88	X	120	x
57	9	89	Y	121	y
58	:	90	Z	122	z
59	;	91	[	123	{
60	<	92	\	124		
61	=	93	]	125	}
62	>	94	^	126	~
63	?	95	_		

CHARACTER ENTITIES

The solution to both of these scenarios is something called **character entities**. To use these you type a special little bit of code into the HTML text which, when rendered, will be displayed as the desired character. All special characters and many extended characters have their own dedicated character entity.

How to Write a Character Entity

Character entities consist of an ampersand '&' followed by an entity name, such as 'quot', and are rounded off with a semicolon ';'. So, to create a quote character, we type " rather than typing an actual quote mark. Interestingly, because an ampersand is itself a special character, you have to write & to make one appear in the rendered text of your page.

```
26      <body>
27          <header>
28              <h1>Special Characters</h1>
29          </header>
30          <section>
31              <p>&quot;There are many special characters in HTML&quot; said the man. &quot;
        Characters such as '&lt;' &amp; '&gt;' can't be typed directly into the text of an HTML
        document.&quot; he said.</p>
32              <p>He went on to explain that the same was true of &quot;extended&quot;
        characters such as &copy;, &micro; and many more. Accented latin characters, such as '
        &Aacute;' and '&Egrave;' are also classed as extended characters, he explained.</p>
33          </section>
34
35      </body>
```

Above: All special and many extended characters are represented by character entities.

Unnamed Entities

Not all extended characters have a predefined character entity, so how do we include such a character in a page? This time we have to use a character code reference instead of an entity name – it looks like this: &#x00A9 ; (this would be a '©' character). The '#' states that what follows is a character code and the 'x' states that the code is being supplied in **Unicode** format. A discussion of Unicode is beyond the scope of this book, but you can look up the code for any character at http://unicode-table.com/en/.

Hot Tip

There are many different character entity names. If your HTML editor supports code hinting then this will help you find the one you want. Otherwise, keep a bookmark somewhere handy that points to http://dev.w3.org/html5/html-author/charref.

```
26      <body>
27          <header>
28              <h1>Special Characters</h1>
29          </header>
30          <section>
31              <p>&quot;There are many special characters in HTML&quot; said the man. &quot;
    Characters such as '&lt;' &amp; '&' can't be typed directly into the text of an HTML
    document.&quot; he said.</p>
32              <p>He went on to expla        was true of &quot;extended&quot;
    characters such as &copy;, &micro;        Accented latin characters, such as '
    &Aacute;' and '&Egrave;' are also        ded characters, he explained.</p>
33          </section>
34
35      </body>
```

Above: Code hinting can be a huge help in finding the desired character entity.

ADAPTIVE LAYOUTS

Building websites is no longer a case of creating a website that looks good on a desktop computer. Mobile devices – smartphones and tablets – are now widely used for web browsing, and this has an impact on how we lay out and style web pages.

```
10          body {
11              font-family:"Lato";
12              font-size:14px;
13          }
14
15          #wrapper {
16              width:80%;
17              height:auto;
18              margin-left:auto;
19              margin-right:auto;
20          }
21
22          section {
23              width:70%;
24              height:auto;
25              float:left;
26          }
27
28          aside {
29              width:30%;
30              float:left;
31          }
32
33          footer {
34              width:100%;
35              height:auto;
36              float:left;
37              background-color:lightgray;
38              border-top:1px solid gray;
39              padding-left:1%;
40              padding-bottom:1%;
41          }
```

FIT TO ALL SCREENS

There are several options when it comes to making a site for all screens, big and small. One approach that has been around since the early days of the internet is proportional – *aka* 'liquid' – layouts. When using this technique we express positions and dimensions in percentage terms. This causes the layout to scale to the size of the browser window.

Left: Expressing dimensions and positions as percentages is one way to make your pages adapt to the browser window's dimensions.

CREATING A LIQUID LAYOUT

When creating a `<div>` or other structural element, it is common to specify a width for it in absolute terms, for example, 1000px ('px' is the code you use in CSS to denote pixels). If the browser window's width is less than this then some of the page will spill over the edges and won't be visible without scrolling.

Stating sizes in percentages solves this problem to a certain degree because it keeps things in proportion: if a `<div>` element's width is set to 80% then it will always be 80 per cent of the width of its containing block. Throw together a few coloured `<div>` elements in a page to see how this works.

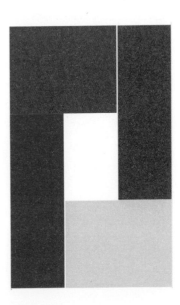

Above & below: This arrangement of `<div>` elements highlights how liquid layouts work.

```
 2
 3  <html>
 4
 5      <head>
 6          <title>Untitled Document</title>
 7      </head>
 8
 9      <body>
10
11          <header>
12              <!--The header element's containing block is the body element-->
13
14              <p>This p element's containing block is the header element</p>
15
16              <p>This is an inline image: <img src="images/myImage.jpg"/>
17                  it's a child of the p element</p>
18              <!--The containing block of the img element is also the
19              header because a p doesn't form a block-->
20
21          </header>
22
23      </body>
24
25  </html>
26
```

Above: Every visual element has a containing block that is used as the reference point for sizing and positioning.

Hot Tip

An element's containing block is the nearest ancestor of that element that can be used as a reference point for sizing and positioning.

Problems with Liquid Layouts

The liquid layout technique was developed at a time before mobile devices and was intended to cope with the lower resolution monitors that computers tended to have back then. It is becoming something of a relic, though, because modern monitors are normally perfectly big enough to accommodate the largest of designs. Liquid layouts do not work especially well on mobile devices either; this being due to the way such devices internally manage screen scaling. The modern approach, then, is to craft your page so that it will display well on *any* device whether mobile or desktop.

RESPONSIVE WEB DESIGN

> Responsive Web Design, also known as RWD, is a technique for making a page or site adapt automatically to the type and size of device on which it is being viewed.

MEDIA QUERIES

Responsive Web Design is powered by what are known as **media queries**. These are a component of CSS that allow you to use values that aren't determined until the page is loaded into a browser. So instead of setting a `<header>` element to be, say, 1000 pixels wide, you could set it to always match the width of the browser window, no matter how wide that window, like this:

```
header {width:device-width;}
```

Below: The Boston Globe's website is one of the original examples of Responsive Web Design.

DIFFERENT DEVICES, DIFFERENT STYLE SHEETS

Desktop, tablet and smartphone screens are all of different widths and resolutions. The way to deal with this is to create multiple versions of a style sheet, each one tailored to support a specific class of device. The browser will then select a sheet based on the `<style>`/`<link>` element's media attribute value.

```
 8
 9          <link
10              rel="stylesheet"
11              type="text/css"
12              href="handheldSmall.css"
13              media="handheld and max-device-width:480px"
14          />
15
16          <link
17              rel="stylesheet"
18              type="text/css"
19              href="handheldLarge.css"
20              media="handheld and min-device-width:481px"
21          />
22
23          <style media="all and not handheld">
24
25
26              body {
27                  font-family:"Lato";
28                  font-size:14px;
29              }
30
31              #wrapper {
32                  width:1000px;
33                  height:auto;
```

Above: The browser can select a style sheet based on the type of device it is running on.

Same Meat, Different Gravy

The various style sheets will all contain the same selectors, and the same style properties will be used in each selector's style rule. What will be different are the values assigned to the style properties. This means that the entire layout of your page will adapt itself to the user's device.

GETTING HELP TO GO RESPONSIVE

There are a number of frameworks available that will take much of the hard work out of the process of building your own RWD site, so if you want to try your hand at it then check out the following tools.

FRAMEWORKS

The two most popular and best-featured RWD frameworks are Foundation and Bootstrap. They provide all of the necessary resources required to build an RWD site: menus, image sliders, buttons and much more. Take a look at both to see which you prefer.

Above: Get started with Bootstrap by downloading and experimenting with it (http://getbootstrap.com).

Responsive Templates

Frameworks are the perfect solution for those who want to create a responsive website, but you still need to learn how to use them. A simpler and quicker solution is to use ready-made templates, leaving you with little more to do than add text and images to create a complete site. Try HTML5 UP (http://html5up.net) for some modern templates.

RWD Tool to Try

When creating a website, it's essential to test it on as many screens as possible, but with the plethora of different screen sizes out there this is not always feasible. There are many tools that can help by simulating different device screens on your desktop. Screenfly is a great example of such a tool; check it out at http://quirktools.com/screenfly.

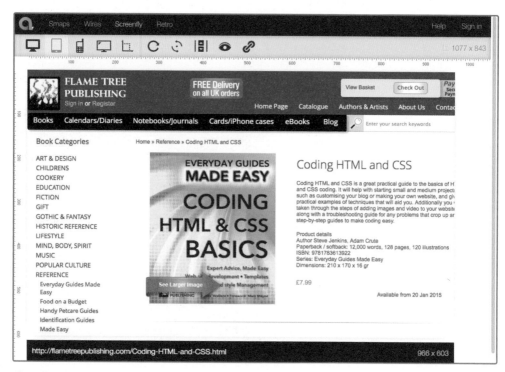

Above: Test a live site on myriad devices and screens.

CONTROLLING MOBILE BROWSER SCALING

Web browsers running on mobile devices behave quite differently to a desktop browser when it comes to sizing a page. This is due to the way in which mobile devices scale between their physical resolution and an internal viewport size.

THE VIEWPORT

A mobile browser's viewport is the area in which it renders the visual content of the page. When the page loads, this viewport is scaled with the aim of making the viewport fit within the physical dimensions of the device's screen. When you zoom in and out with a nip of your fingers, you're actually adjusting the viewport scaling, and when you scroll around the page you're actually moving the viewport around.

Right: The viewport can, and often does, extend beyond the visible area of the screen.

The Viewport Meta Tag

In order to have the browser adopt a suitable initial scaling for the viewport, we have to let it know what size we want it to assume; if we don't do this then a default value will be used which may or may not be suitable. We set the scaling via a `<meta>` tag placed in the `<head>` of the page.

Viewport Properties

The thing we are interested in is the value of the `content` attribute. This is used to set a viewport property; in our example we are telling the viewport to match the physical width of the device. Available properties are: `width`, `height`, `minimum-scale`, `maximum-scale`, `initial-scale` and `user-scalable`.

```
5   <head>
6
7       <meta name="viewport" content="width=device-width">
8
9       <title>My First Web Page</title>
```

Above: The viewport meta tag defines the initial scaling employed by a mobile browser.

BROWSER SUPPORT

There is a host of browsers for desktop and mobile, all offering different levels of support for HTML5 and CSS3. On the desktop the major browsers are Chrome, Firefox, Internet Explorer and Safari, so you should aim to test all of your sites in at least these four browsers.

WHICH BROWSERS SHOULD I SUPPORT?

There is no doubt that Chrome, Firefox, Internet Explorer, Safari and even Opera should be supported on the desktop. The question is which version should you support? As a general rule, encourage visitors to your site to install and use the latest version of their preferred browser(s).

Hot Tip

Download and install the main browsers so that you can test your pages in each one.

Browser Compatibility Test		Web Design Gallery		Icon Search Engine	

Enter URL Here: www.bbc.co.uk   Submit

△ Linux	⊿ Windows			Mac	⚡ BSD
☐ Arora 0.1	☑ Iceape 2.7	☑ Chrome 10.0	☑ Chrome 35.0	☑ Firefox 17.0	☑ Camino 2.1
☑ Arora 0.11	☑ Iceweasel 3.5	☑ Chrome 12.0	☑ Chrome 36.0	☑ Firefox 18.0	☑ Chrome 34.0
☑ Chrome 27.0	☑ Kazehakase 0.5	☑ Chrome 13.0	☑ Firefox 1.5	☑ Firefox 19.0	☑ Chrome 35.0
☑ Chrome 30.0	☑ Konqueror 4.11	☑ Chrome 14.0	☑ Firefox 2.0	☑ Firefox 20.0	☑ Firefox 25.0
☑ Chrome 31.0	☑ Konqueror 4.4	☑ Chrome 17.0	☐ Firefox 3.0	☑ Firefox 21.0	☑ Firefox 26.0
☑ Chrome 35.0	☑ Konqueror 4.8	☑ Chrome 18.0	☑ Firefox 3.5	☑ Firefox 22.0	☑ Firefox 27.0
☑ Chrome 37.0	☑ Konqueror 4.9	☑ Chrome 19.0	☑ Firefox 4.0	☑ Firefox 23.0	☑ Firefox 28.0
☑ Dillo 3.0	☑ Links 2.7	☑ Chrome 20.0	☑ Firefox 5.0	☑ Firefox 24.0	☑ Firefox 29.0
☑ Epiphany 3.10	☐ Luakit 1.1	☑ Chrome 21.0	☑ Firefox 6.0	☑ Firefox 25.0	☑ Firefox 30.0
☑ Epiphany 3.4	☐ Luakit 1.6	☑ Chrome 22.0	☑ Firefox 7.0	☑ Firefox 26.0	☑ Firefox 31.0
☑ Epiphany 3.6	☑ Luakit 1.8	☑ Chrome 23.0	☑ Firefox 8.0	☑ Firefox 27.0	☑ Firefox 32.0
☐ Firefox 3.0	☑ Lynx 2.8	☑ Chrome 24.0	☑ Firefox 9.0	☑ Firefox 28.0	☑ Opera 21.0

Contribute

Free 7-Day Trial
- Largest set of VM machines anywhere
- Test your site in as few as two clicks

CrossBrowserTesting

Above: A browser compatibility tool like Browsershots can help you test your site.

TROUBLESHOOTING COMMON PROBLEMS

When working with web-based technologies, there will always be issues of compatibility. Here we run through some of the common issues that you are likely to encounter when building websites.

WEB PAGE DOESN'T DISPLAY PROPERLY IN INTERNET EXPLORER

Older versions of Internet Explorer use a different method to other browsers to display certain HTML and CSS elements. However, the latest versions of Internet Explorer are much more standards-compliant than previous ones. The best workaround is to keep code as simple as possible.

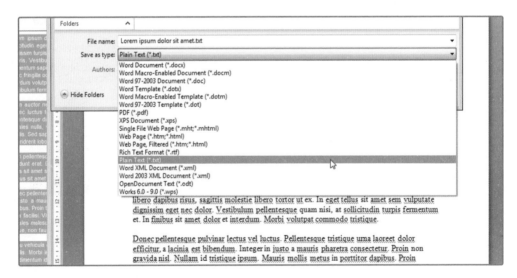

Above: Save Word documents as plain text before copying into an HTML page.

COPYING TEXT FROM WORD LEAVES LOADS OF EXTRA TEXT

Copying text directly from a Word document into a web page will also bring in a load of the styling that Word applies to its documents. You could delete this by hand, but this is time-consuming. A simple solution is to save the Word document as a text-only file and then copy and paste the text into a web page.

WHY ISN'T MY IMAGE SHOWING?

There could be a number of reasons but the first port of call is to make sure that the image's URL is using the correct path, name and file extension. You might be using a URL with the right image name but the wrong file extension, for example, png instead of jpg, or not have provided the correct folder path information.

HOW DO I CHECK THAT MY HTML IS CORRECT?

The best way to check your HTML and CSS for errors is to use an online validation tool such as the official W3C validator at http://validator.w3.org/. If you use an HTML editor such as Dreamweaver to build your pages, it will have validation tools built in.

Above: Use a validation tool or service to test your HTML.

WHY ISN'T MY CODE WORKING ON MY DESKTOP?

You might have all your HTML and CSS in place and working well, but when you add some new code and test on your desktop find that nothing happens. The first step is to check that any code or scripts are pointing to the right location. If all is fine in that department, upload the page to your web server and test it from there — some code only works when it is running from a server.

IMAGES ARE LOADING VERY SLOWLY

It is not uncommon for users to place images with large file sizes onto a web page and then resize them with CSS. Multiply this by ten images and everything slows to a crawl.

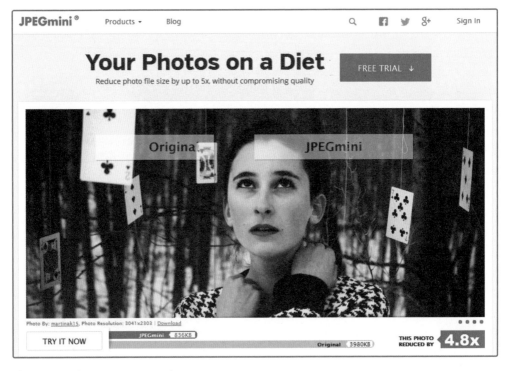

Above: Use an online image optimizer to reduce image sizes.

Try optimizing any images you are using; if you don't have an image editor then the JPEGmini online service will do the trick – *http://www.jpegmini.com.*

SOME OF MY LINKS AREN'T WORKING

Links are critical to site navigation, and so broken links can be a big problem. The first thing to check is that the `<a>` element and its `href` attribute's URL are both written correctly – if there is one mistake in the URL it won't work. If you are using a relative URL then changing to an absolute one (starting with http://) can solve the problem.

FONT ISSUES

Computers come with fonts such as Arial, Helvetica and Georgia installed. However, if you are using a different font it may not be available on the user's computer and so a substitute will be used. Web fonts get around this, but the correct code must be added in the right place. Use Google Fonts – *https://www.google.com/fonts* – for peace of mind.

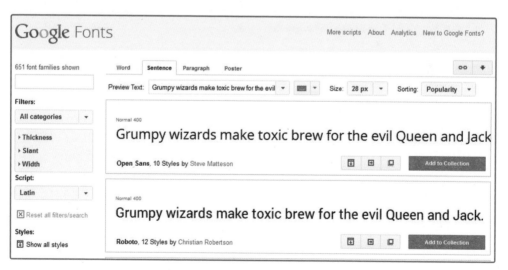

Above: Google Fonts offers hundreds of different fonts.

ONLINE RESOURCES

The web provides a vast array of tools, libraries and information to make creating web pages and websites a more productive experience. Here we are going to list some of the more useful resources found online.

HTML RESOURCES

W3C

The World Wide Web Consortium is the body responsible for all web standards. Its site is packed with information from simple guides to deeply technical whitepapers.
http://www.w3.org

Mozilla Developer Network

This resource is run by Mozilla, the creators of the Firefox browser. It offers a quick introduction to HTML and links to a comprehensive reference library.
**https://developer.mozilla.org/
en-US/docs/Web/HTML**

HTML5 Rocks

Lots of articles and tutorials. Aimed at the more advanced user of HTML, but still very useful.
http://www.html5rocks.com/en/

CSS RESOURCES

CSS3 Info

The latest news, previews and working examples of CSS3.
http://www.css3.info

W3Schools

A comprehensive guide with the option to test your code online.
http://www.w3schools.com/css/

Above: W3Schools has a host of learning resources

BEST FRAMEWORKS

Foundation

Touted as 'the most advanced responsive front-end framework in the world', Foundation provides all the components needed for a responsive website.
http://foundation.zurb.com/

Bootstrap

The most popular front-end responsive framework used on thousands of sites.
http://getbootstrap.com/

INDEX

A

absolute URLs 58
Adobe Dreamweaver 69, 123
Adobe Flash Player 28
Adobe Illustrator 69
Adobe Photoshop 29, 88, 69
American Standard Code for
    Information Interchange see
    ASCII
anchor element 57–58
animations 30
    apply an animation 100
    creating a simple animation 101–
    102
article elements 45
ASCII 109
aside elements 45
attributes 12, 13, 24, 33
    class attributes 47
    id attribute 39
audio formats 95

B

backgrounds 30
blocks, containing 113–14
blogs 82
    Wordpress.com 82–83
    Wordpress.org 83
body elements 20
Bootstrap 117, 126
Brackets 68
browser support 121
    mobile browsers 119–20
browsers
    Chrome 121
    Firefox 121
    Internet Explorer 121
    Opera 121
    Safari 121

C

Cascading Style Sheets see CSS
character codes 109
character entities 110
    how to write a character
        entity 110
    unnamed entities 111
child elements 16–17,56
child selectors 50
Chrome 121
Class selectors 15, 46
    class attributes 47
    multiple classification 48
    Typed Class selectors 47
CoffeeCup Free HTML Editor 68
compound selectors 49–50

containing blocks 113–14
content 43
CorelDRAW 69
Crute, Adam Coding JavaScript
    Basics 105
CSS 7, 33
    checking with W3C 123
    Class selectors 46–48
    components 17
    compound selectors 49–50
    CSS keyframes 100–102
    CSS transforms 98
    CSS transitions 98–99
    embedded style sheets 22, 26,
        33, 75
    expertise 31–33
    external style sheets 22–23, 25,
        26, 33, 75
    linking CSS documents to HTML
        documents 24–25
    multiple style sheets 25–26
    online resources 126
    structure 16–17
    styling a page with CSS 75–79
    what does CSS look like? 15
    what is CSS? 14–15
    why isn't my code working on
        my desktop? 124
CSS3 29
    animations 30
    better backgrounds 30
    CSS shadow 29
    visual effects 29–30
CSS3 Info 126
CyberDuck 81

D

default pages 71
default style sheets 59
definition lists 63
descendant selectors 49
div element 38–39, 40, 42
DOCTYPE declaration 18–19
domain name 80
drag-and-drop 97
Dreamweaver 69, 123

E

elements 10, 12, 33, 37
    anchor element 57–58
    child elements 16–17, 56
    code comments 21
    containing blocks 114
    content 43
    div element 38–39, 40, 42
    DOCTYPE declaration 18–19
    footer elements 43
    head and body elements 20
    header elements 42

heading text 51–54
    HTML element 19
    iframe element 94
    img element 89–91
    modifying elements 12
    paragraph text 55–56
    parent elements 16–17
    script element 104
    semantic elements 27–28,
        40–41
    structural elements 44–45
    what's inside an element 11
embedded style sheets 22, 26,
        33, 75
expertise 31
    basics 33
    faster websites 32
    JavaScript 105
    keeping up with trends 32
    site modification 32
extended characters 109
external style sheets 22–23, 26,
        33, 75
    advantages 25

F

File Transfer Protocol (FTP) 81
Filezilla 81
Firefox 121
folders 70
    creating a basic structure 71–74
    site root folders 24
fonts 76, 78
    font issues 125
footer elements 43
forms 96
Foundation 117, 126
frameworks 117, 126
    responsive templates 118
    Screenfly 118
FTP (File Transfer Protocol) 81

G

geolocation 97
Google Fonts 125

H

head elements 20, 42
header elements 42
heading text 51
    heading groups 54
    heading levels 52
    heading semantics 52–53
    logical structure of headings 53
hot tips 7
    adding video 93
    animation 100, 101
    browsers 121
    character codes 109

character entities 111
child elements 56
Class selectors 47
code comments 21
containing blocks 114
CSS structure 17
default pages 71
default style sheets 59
folders 70
fonts 76, 78
head and header elements 42
heading text 51
id attribute 39
image formats 88
menu/navigation system 43
Ogg-Vorbis formats 95
page semantics 73
page width 79
quote marks in HTML 12
site root folders 24
TextEdit 68
unordered lists 62
visual effects 30
HTML 6, 33
    adding a video with HTML 93
    checking with Dreamweaver 123
    checking with W3C 123
    code comments 21
    components of HTML 12
    doing things with style 13
    expertise 31–33
    how do I check that my HTML is
        correct? 123
    HTML editors 69
    linking CSS documents to HTML
        documents 24–25
    modifying elements 12
    special characters 108–109
    what does HTML look like? 11
    what is HTML? 10
    why isn't my code working on
        my desktop? 124
HTML5 27
    drag-and-drop 97
    forms 96
    geolocation 97
    mobiles 28
    new functionality 28
    semantic elements 27–28, 40–41
HTML5 Rocks 126
hyperlinks 57
    anchor element 57–58
    creating a hyperlink 58
    opening a hyperlink in a new
        window 60
    some of my links aren't
        working 125
    styling links 59–60
    URLs 58

HyperText Markup Language
  see HTML

I
id attribute 39
ID selectors 15, 40
iDraw 69
iframe element 94
Illustrator 69
image editors 69
  image and graphics editor links 69
image formats 87
  JPG format 88
  PNG format 87
images 86
  how to add an image 89–91
  images are loading very slowly
    124–25
  why isn't my image showing? 123
inline style 14, 26, 33
Internet Explorer 121
  web page doesn't display properly
    in Internet Explorer 122

J
JavaScript 96, 103
  adding a script 104
  execute on sight 105
  expertise 105
  script element 104
  where does JavaScript fit?
    103–105
JPG format 88

K
keyframes 100–102

L
layouts 112
  creating a liquid layout 113–14
  fit to all screens 112
  problems with liquid layouts 114
lists 61
  definition lists 63
  list items 61
  lists within lists 63
  ordered lists 63
  unordered lists 62

M
menus 43
mobile browsers 119
  viewport 119
  viewport meta tag 120
  viewport properties 120
mobile devices 28, 119
Mozilla Developer Network 126
MP3 formats 95
multiple classification 48

multiple style sheets 25–26
  methods of applying styling 26
multiple Type selectors 49

N
navigation systems 43
Notepad 68
Notepad++ 68

O
Ogg-Vorbis formats 95
online 80
  adding a blog to your site 82–83
  domain name 80
  online resources 126
  transferring files 81
  web server 81
  Wordpress.com 82–83
  Wordpress.org 83
Opera 121
ordered lists 63

P
page sections 44
page width 79
Paint Shop Pro 69
paragraph text 55
  styling paragraphs 55
  styling within a paragraph 56
parent elements 16–17
Photoshop 29, 88, 69
Pixelmator 69
planning 66
  what should a sketch include?
    66–67
PNG (Portable Network Graphics)
  format 87
Pseudo-Class selectors 59, 60, 99

R
relative URLs 58
Responsive Web Design
  (RWD) 115
  different devices, different style
    sheets 116
  frameworks 117–18
  media queries 115

S
Safari 121
Screenfly 118
script element 104
selectors 15, 17, 33
  child selectors 50
  Class selectors 15, 46–48
  descendant selectors 49
  ID selectors 15, 40
  Pseudo-Class selectors 59,
    60, 99

selection of selectors 15
  Type selectors 15, 47
  Typed Class selectors 47
semantic elements 27–28, 40–41
  page semantics 73
site navigation 43, 44
site root folders 24
sketching 66
  what should a sketch include?
    66–67
special characters 108
  ASCII and extended
    characters 109
style commands 13
style properties 13, 17, 33
style rules 13, 17, 33
style sheets
  default style sheets 59
  different devices, different style
    sheets 116
  embedded style sheets 22, 26,
    33, 75
  external style sheets 22–23, 25,
    26, 33, 75
  multiple style sheets 25–26
styling a page 75
  creating the CSS code 75–79
  embedded or external style
    sheets 75
styling links 59
  Pseudo-Class electors 60
Sublime Text 68

T
tags 10, 12, 33
  closing tags 11
  opening tags 11
text editors 68
  Brackets 68
  CoffeeCup Free HTML Editor 68
  Notepad 68
  Notepad++ 68
  Sublime Text 68
  TextEdit 68
  TopStyle5 68
transferring files 81
transforms 98
transitions 98
  how transitions work 99
troubleshooting 122
  copying text from Word leaves
    loads of extra text 123
  font issues 125
  how do I check that my HTML is
    correct? 123
  images are loading very slowly
    124–25
  some of my links aren't
    working 125

web page doesn't display properly
  in Internet Explorer 122
  why isn't my code working on my
    desktop? 124
  why isn't my image showing? 123
'tweening' 101
Type selectors 15, 47
  multiple Type selectors 49

U
unordered lists 62
URLs (Uniform Resource
  Locators) 58

V
video 92
  adding a video with HTML 93
  adding a YouTube video 94
visual impairment 27

W
W3C 126
  checking HTML and CSS 123
W3Schools 126
web servers 81
websites 6–7
  adaptive layouts 112–14
  adding audio 95
  adding images 89–92
  adding video 92–94
  basic build 36–37
  creating a wireframe 67
  creating a working folder 70–74
  faster websites 32
  HTML editors 69
  image editors 69
  image formats 87–88
  keeping up with trends 32
  planning and sketching 66–67
  site modification 32
  styling a page with CSS 75–79
  text editors 68
  working with images 86
wireframes 67
WordPress 7
  Wordpress.com 82–83
  Wordpress.org 83

X
XHTML 18, 19

Y
YouTube videos 94
  iframe element 94